Ben Martin's
FLEXIBLE T
OFFENSE

Ben Martin's
FLEXIBLE T
OFFENSE

BEN MARTIN
Head Football Coach,
United States
Air Force Academy

ENGLEWOOD CLIFFS, N.J.
PRENTICE-HALL, INC.

PRINTED IN THE UNITED STATES OF AMERICA

07320—BC

Foreword

This book, the same as any other project involving a complex game like modern American football, is not the effort of any one man. The author has been fortunate to have extremely capable young men on his staff at the Air Force Academy. All of these men have contributed a great deal to the compilation of the material as presented. Prior to the project of writing a book, the staff contributed their original ideas in the creation of the Flexible T offense, displaying strong indications of a basic understanding of all phases of this great game.

Thanks and appreciation are extended to the entire football coaching staff of the Academy with special recognition to John Ignarski, Tom Berry, Gene Blasi, Frank Ellwood, Tom Bakke and Pepper Rodgers.

BEN MARTIN

Ben Martin's Flexible T Offense

Ben Martin's
FLEXIBLE T
OFFENSE

1

Keeping the "Game" in Football

It is hoped that this book will convey some usable ideas about offensive football to coaches and students of the great game as well as interesting information to readers in general.

There are almost as many offensive approaches to football as there are teams playing. There are systems galore, plays by the hundreds and players of great and little ability. The offensive series, the play patterns, whether they be runs or passes, are the weapons to be used. We will detail these patterns and show how they can best be used in a game.

Football: A Game of People

We believe in carefully devised and well-rehearsed patterns, but we also believe that football is more than a series of plays and patterns. These weapons must be controlled by people, and are only as effective as the execution given to them by the players. Football is a game not so much of systems, but of people. Because there will not be space for the author to dwell at length on the human aspect of the game and still give the reader the complete offensive picture, this opening chapter is directed toward the viewpoint of the players.

1

Football is a game. It is meant to be enjoyable for the participants. Coaches should never lose sight of this principle. We are firmly convinced that it is vitally important to keep the "game" in football. Certainly there are phases of football that are hard work, but it doesn't necessarily follow that it be drudgery. All hard work is basically rewarding to the people participating. The young men who comprise the football squad have many personal reasons for playing the game and for striving to improve. At the base of all the reasons, however, it appears they all feel that football will bring them pleasure and satisfaction: the pleasure of playing a game and the satisfaction of accomplishment that comes when men are pitted against each other competitively.

We like to assume that all of the players want to make the team, or else they wouldn't be out for practice. With this basic belief it becomes the coach's task to guide, assist and teach the player in an effort to help him to reach his goal. Each player should strive to make the team and then further strive to be the best player on it.

Whose Team Is It?

With these aims in mind the coach must realize that the team belongs to the players and the school they represent. The coach can only hope to claim that he, too, is "on the team," and not that it belongs to him. He will necessarily, because of his position of responsibility, share many deep and valuable human emotional experiences with the players.

This aspect of the game of football is one of its greatest values; for through participation, the team members experience just about the entire range of human emotion in a controlled, game atmosphere. The exalted joy of a victory gained at the last second; the deep warm satisfaction of a job won by concentrated effort and determination from start to finish; and the deep despair, the agony, of a vitally important contest lost by some seeming unfair act of fate or unexpected human error —these are the emotions that a coach shares with his players, and he must understand their personal reactions to each one. Some of the players must be driven, some need to be relaxed and others to be left alone. Throughout the entire range of human relations the strength of discipline must prevail; firm but fair. It will give the players the strength of unity and weld them into a team.

Variety, Humor Keep Enthusiasm High

Variety is truly the spice of life and humor is universal. To maintain interest and the high morale of the players, a coach should always have his eye on these two helpers. Variety will result in a high level of performance and participation. Interest will remain keen and workouts will be lively. Since football is a game, humor and fun is surely not out of place. The sharing of a teammate's humorous misfortune or a truly comical situation that develops from an ordinary practice routine is a welcome relief from the arduous chores of preparing for a game. Just as authors in creating fiction must spice a story with comic relief, so must a coach enliven his practices or suffer the dire results of boredom among the players.

In analyzing the situation and prescribing the use of humor, care must be taken to ascertain that levity and frivolity do not usurp the basic tone of seriousness of purpose so necessary to success. There is a time for the light touch and a time for the deadly serious, dedicated approach of the true competitor. Just as some great golfers can be light-hearted and personable while walking down the fairway between shots, but then clam up, almost to the point of being grim, once they address the ball —so can a football player use changing moods to his advantage.

Along with variety comes its companion in sports activity—

competition. As many of the practice drills and exercises as possible should be made competitive. The participants will develop much faster and improve their skills more rapidly through the challenge of competition. Their will to excel is sharpened by it.

Before plunging ahead into the system of offensive football that follows, it is well to mention the cardinal sin of over-coaching. It is generally better that an athlete be under-coached. Yet it takes a constant effort on the part of most coaches if they are to coach a player just right.

The Natural Approach to Football

We believe in the "natural way" of playing football. By this we mean that the personal skills and talents of each player should be recognized, developed and used to their fullest effectiveness. They should be used within the team framework and the general philosophy of attack; but not forced into a pattern which is unnatural to the individual. Your team will have its own personality but it will be the sum of all the individual personalities on the team. *Know them.*

How well we remember seeing a player punt the ball 60 yards early in pre-season practice. But he kicked with an inconsistent drop of the ball and with a leg that was bent at the knee. After being coached on a steady drop and a straight leg, the player's punt traveled only 45 yards! This result is what we want, isn't it? What's wrong with kicking with a poor drop or a bent knee as long as the ball travels 60 yards? That's over-coaching. Just keep that 60-yard kicker happy. This doesn't mean to say that a beginner, or ineffectual punter should be taught to kick other than with a consistent drop and straight leg; but leave well enough alone—don't over-coach.

The "natural way" also means that a ball carrier, who can gain valuable yardage on the strength of his natural skills to find a hole to run through, should not be forbidden to run to "daylight." We have known backs who were schooled to run a spot, say off-tackle, and finding a pile of players there and no hole, were not permitted to run elsewhere, even though the chance of success was much greater anyplace but at the off-tackle spot. Our backs are permitted to, *encouraged* to, run to daylight as the play develops because the result is what is de-sired—gained yardage.

In this same approach, a lineman is not asked to block a man the hard way. That is, if the opponent is aligned to our line-man's left, our player is not required to block him to his right. This command could be very frustrating as well as impossible if the opponent has about equal ability. Our player would be asked to block the opponent any way that is convenient; but block him, and the ball carrier will run to daylight—the "natural way."

This book will present an entire and complete system of offen-sive football. We have found it to be an offense with all the needed weapons. It is hoped that some parts of it can be adapted to other systems, perhaps to fill a void or to add a useful weapon. We believe that all systems are good as long as they are based upon fundamental theories that have been proved through suc-cessful use. Once the fundamentals are recognized and estab-lished, you have a real opportunity to create a system which will augment the personal abilities of your players and provide them with the weapons they need to be successful.

2

Evaluating Players and Selecting the Team

Picking the Squad

IT STANDS TO REASON that the best product can only be made by using the very best raw materials available to the manufacturer. The same principle applies to the production of the best possible football team. Here the main raw materials are the players. We all could pick a dream-team from recognized players and thus have the needed raw material; but this is not the problem that confronts most coaches. Their problem is to assemble a squad and evaluate the players in order to: (1) reduce the number to a workable size, and (2) determine just who the best players are.

We all have the problem of determining who the best players are. We want to make sure that we are fielding the most skillful and productive team from those who comprise the squad. Maybe we can't do anything about the type and number of players who come out for the team, but we certainly can evaluate them and play those who rate highest.

It becomes important, too, that coaching staffs are not swamped by so many applicants that they are unable to give them the benefit of their teaching skills. Thus it is well to consider cutting the squad to a reasonable number. Our approach is to keep on the team all of those athletes who have the potential to play in a game. If we need more than that number (which is usually the case) in order to have enough units to organize a practice session, then we retain the sophomore and junior class members whose physical assets would make them most valuable in helping to prepare the varsity players for a game.

We would retain the sophomores and juniors rather than seniors in this capacity, because of the many menial tasks asked of them and the relatively small chance they have to progress to varsity caliber in one year. We have also found that the younger boys, with physical assets, learn surprisingly fast when put under the gun regularly against good opposition. They seem to suddenly see the light, and mature quickly. What a gratifying experience it is for a coach to find that last year's scrub is this year's regular—all unexpected depth.

Those retained, but not of immediate potential, should have certain physical assets, as mentioned, in order to be of most benefit to the varsity. For instance, the scrubs may be asked to imitate the next week's opponent team, so the linemen should have some size, at least at tackle. This gives the varsity a better picture of what to expect. It would be less than productive to drill your first team against a line of 130-pound cast-off guards, even though those little fellows are your scrappiest scrubs. They usually have more immediate potential than some of the more adequately equipped retainees, but their future growth as players is often extremely limited.

A method for selection of players will be outlined as will the attributes that are considered to be of paramount importance. It is well never to lose sight of the fact that the boys you have on the squad are the only ones from whom you can draw for a starting eleven. So, pick the best players and play them. This usually involves switching positions for some. A real player wants to be in the contest, and if he seems reluctant to change

positions, he can easily be convinced that it's better to be playing at the new position than watching from the old. He will also
come around quickly and discover that all spots on a team are
fun if you're a football player.

Desirable Attributes of a Football Player

What makes a good football player? This is a simple question; but the answer is fairly complex. How many times have
you heard said of an accomplished player, "Why he doesn't even
look like a football player!" Or, "Why doesn't that boy play
on the team, he certainly looks like a football player." As is the
case with just about every activity of human participation, it's
not always what is obvious to see that is important to success.
Most often it's what's inside the heart and mind of the man.

This is certainly true of the football player, and the inner
workings of his heart and mind, vitally important to his success as
a player, are most difficult to fathom. As a coach, you must be
able to evaluate the human intangibles which will play so big a
role in the success of your team—such characteristics as courage,
determination, aggressiveness and the ability to make the right
decision—judgment, or football I.Q., if you will. Let's take a
closer look at definitions for these intangibles.

1. COURAGE—Because of the inescapable fact that football is
a contact sport, it follows that the players should be courageous.
Those who are fearless and love contact are easiest defined. They
look for the contact and never seem to get enough of it. It would
be well if the entire squad were composed of fearless lovers of
body contact. But this is usually not the case. There are courageous athletes who can take or leave the contact, or whose
hunger for it comes in spurts. Some really have it during a game
when the opposition becomes the true enemy. This type can be
a real effective player if not over-exposed to the basic contact
phases of the game.

Perhaps the most difficult type is the one who apparently looks the part of a player, but who shies from contact. He is difficult to distinguish from the one who is fearful and not courageous, the one who really doesn't want anything to do with contact under any circumstances. There is no place on a football team for an athlete who is always concerned about his physical safety, who is afraid of being bruised or injured by contact. He is a liability. But there is a place for the aspirant who seemingly lacks courage because of naiveté and ignorance. He is not afraid, but fails to realize the impression he is giving to his coach and to his squad mates.

This boy can be trained, step by step, to display the native courage that he has. Be careful to lead him through what can be a tremendous ordeal, but can also make a man of him. Do not overwhelm him with a task that calls for a great display of courage at first. Do not corner him before he understands and knows how to fight his way out. Explain the facts of contact-sport life to him—"It's easiest when you strike first and hardest."

We feel that many a player can be salvaged from the scrap heap of apparent fear of injury, by the simple process of teaching him to put his head into the fray—figuratively and physically. To accomplish this, you don't ask him to put his head into a hornets' nest or a buzz saw! He'd never want to do that a second time. Have him (fully protected by helmet and face bar) start by gently pushing his face into a soft blocking pad, then harder and harder into the same pad. Then the same approach with a blocking dummy. If he shows progress, not ducking or shying away, go one step further. Let him smash into a passive player, then a controlled action opponent. If he has progressed well to this point, then give him some "live bait" to build his confidence. Let him fly full speed into an opponent of about equal or less ability. Remember that the technique of blocking is not the aspect that is important in this drill. All that is wanted is a fearless approach to contact. The niceties of technique can only be taught after the player has forgotten that he was timid about contact. Show him the fun of it and he'll be a prospect for the team.

2. DETERMINATION—All of the key words in the following general definition of determination have meaning as the word is used as a positive characteristic of a good football player: "Determination is the definite direction of the mind or will towards an objective." It brings into focus the mental aspect of the game, for determination is basically a mental process—making up your mind that you will accomplish a goal. But more than that, it indicates that a "definite direction" has been established.

This is where the coach enters the picture. He can spell out the objective clearly and also define the direction. Once these things have been set forth, the player's will to get the job done takes over. Those who possess strong determination are difficult to discourage. They will try over and over again to accomplish their goal and to please their coaches and teammates. Determined players have a very real purpose. They know where they are going and they are going to get there. There is always room on a team for the determined player.

3. AGGRESSIVENESS—The football player whose character make-up disposes him to initiate the attack, instead of passively waiting for the battle to start, is the aggressive one. He will be an asset to the team. He will be anxious and will prove over and over again that he who hesitates is lost in a football scrimmage. The aggressive player will carry the battle to his opponent and control the valuable momentum of each play. The balance of power will be his and his opponent will have to be concerned about controlling him to a greater degree than he should. The opponent will have the feeling that he is being snowed under by an avalanche or swarmed upon by a horde of bees. He will find it difficult to retain his composure or to play the game at his own pace when he is confronted by an aggressive player.

This aggressiveness will cause a player to be offsides upon

occasion because he is anxious, even over-zealous, to get into combat. But this can be controlled. Woe to the team which has to be driven into battle, the team that has no one who leaps across that scrimmage line occasionally in a premature aggressive move to get at the opposition.

It is much easier for a coach to control and channel the anxious and eager actions of the aggressive player than it is to attempt to spark up the non-aggressors on the team. Look for aggressiveness in your players.

4. FOOTBALL I.Q.—One of the characteristics of the good football player, and perhaps the most intangible of all, is the ability to make the correct decision under duress. Judgment is perhaps closest to its synonym.

The player with a high football I.Q. will anticipate the opponent's action and place himself in an advantageous position to carry out his responsibility. He will make a positive decision quickly as the play develops and will less frequently be caught in the middle, off-balance, and at a disadvantage. His judgment will add up to an efficient use of his native abilities. As all areas of judgment do, the player's football I.Q. will go up a few points with every game he plays, for he will benefit from experience. How often have we all thought, "If I only knew then what I know now, how much better a player I would have been!"

The player with the superior football I.Q. will be at the right place at the right time. He will be the defensive end who closes fast and hard when the play is coming off-tackle. He will be the same player to float with the wide run or drop off to knock down a flat pass. He will be the halfback who cuts back at exactly the correct time to leave his opponent sprawled on the turf, or the blocker who makes contact with an open-field opponent at exactly the right time to permit a long gainer for his team.

Look for the player with the superior football I.Q. He will make those quick efficient decisions during the games just as he does in practice. He is not necessarily the boy with the superior intellect, the one whose academic achievement is best. It is not felt that any realistic correlation exists between I.Q. and *football I.Q.* We have all seen smart boys who are almost dumb footballers, and vice versa. We have also seen the player whose physical attributes appeared inadequate and yet, because of a superior football I.Q., became a great performer.

Natural Ability

We have taken a look at the major intangible qualities that are important in the make-up of a player. Now let us list a few of the more readily recognized attributes, those of a physical, tangible nature. Each player who answers the call for the football squad will have natural attributes which can be readily scrutinized and determined. The ones that we look for in screening candidates, but not necessarily in the order listed, are: (1) Speed and Quickness, (2) Coordination, (3) Strength, and (4) Size.

Of course, it would be most desirable to have players amply provided with all of these characteristics. In practice, however, we usually accept boys who have a bit of each or whose superiority in one aspect makes up for their inadequacy in another. For example, a small player of great speed and quickness can be successful (if used in the right position) despite his lack of size and strength. Conversely, a large strong candidate with little agility can aid the team if used to anchor the defense.

We are looking for:

(1) *Speed* and *Quickness*—The ability to run fast is a decided asset to the player and the coach should be on the lookout for candidates who can move. Since football is usually played in short distance sprints, speed alone is not all that is needed. Perhaps of more significance is quickness, or the ability to get moving instantly. The quick start is vital to all phases of the game.

To determine speed, the very simple expedient of foot races, using a stop watch, is employed. But be careful of racing the candidates before they are properly warmed up. Early-season pulled muscles have a pesky habit of lingering all year. It is recommended that sprints for timing and evaluation be conducted with the players in complete football uniform. There are those whose speed really drops off when they must run in full harness. Others whose speed is coupled with power can run almost as fast when garbed in full equipment (around 15 pounds) as for a game. Since the players will be dressed that way in games when it counts, select them the same way. We believe that sprints of 50 to 75 yards are best to determine speed.

To pick the candidates who have the valuable asset of the fast start but may lack the sustained speed outlined above, limit the sprinting distance to 5 to 15 yards. This test will give a real indication of the player's ability to get going when the ball is snapped.

Without exception, the smaller players must possess speed or quickness if they are to be productive members of a team. These faculties will also keep them out of harm's way and quite capable of surviving the rough-and-tumble that is football.

(2) *Coordination*—On every play in a football game, the players are required to put their bodies through a number of complex movements. For instance, the defensive guard must assume a strong and balanced stance, strike a blow as the ball is snapped, use his hands and arms to protect himself, work his feet to scramble to the ball, resist being tied up or knocked down, and then run to the ball carrier and tackle him. What this player has enacted requires coordination, for coordination is the "combined action of a number of muscles to produce complex movements."

A good football prospect must be coordinated, not clumsy. He must be able to react to what he sees and to the pressures he feels inflicted by the opponent upon his body. He must be able to muster his muscles together to deliver a sharp crisp block as opposed to merely pushing. The coordinated player will be an effective blocker and will be a scrambling defender.

To determine the candidates who possess the coordination required of a good football player, a number of evaluation drills may be used. These drills fall into the area of reaction and agility types and may later be used to develop the same qualities in selected candidates. A successful team must be agile and able to react.

A few suggested drills for all players, regardless of position, are as follows:

a. *Wave Drill* (reaction)

This is an excellent drill for developing reaction, quickness and agility. Each player will complete this drill ten times (five standing and five on all fours).

The coach stands in front of the players and waves his hands in any one of four directions (left, right, back and forward). Normally three players at a time are in action. A player should react at least two times in each direction before completing a turn.

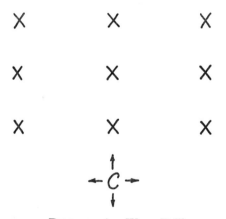

DIAGRAM 1.   Wave Drill.

b. *Scramble Drill*

This drill is used primarily as a warm-up and conditioner. It is a good developer of agility, balance and quickness.

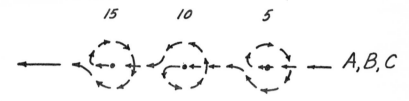

DIAGRAM 2.   Scramble Drill.

Form a single line. Player (A) starts from a three-point stance, sprints five yards, places the inside hand on the ground and completes a 360° circle. He repeats this at least three times, circling in a different direction each time.

c. *Circle Drill*

This drill is designed to develop reaction, aggressiveness and balance. The players form a circle and each is assigned a number. One player is placed in the center of the circle. He will assume a defensive linebacker's stance and as the coach calls a number, he must react to the offender whose number is called. The coach will continue to call a different number until each offender has blocked the defender. At this time, the defender will exchange places with an offender. This drill is repeated until each player has had a turn in the center of the circle.

d. *Triangle Drill*

This drill is used primarily as a reaction drill for linemen. The coach stands behind the defender and signals for either or both of the offenders to shoulder-block the defender. The defender stops the charge of the offender and tries not to be blocked.

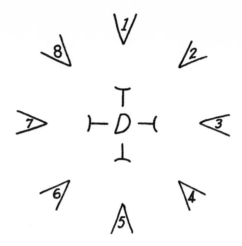

DIAGRAM 3.   Circle Drill.

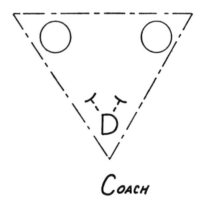

DIAGRAM 4.   Triangle Drill.

e. *Prone Tackling*

This drill can be used for form or full speed tackling. Player (A) lies on his back with knees flexed. Player (B) stands five yards in front of (A) with his back to the tackler. A ball is placed at the feet of (B). On the command, *Hit,* (B) picks up the ball and runs a direct line toward (A). The tackler (A) scrambles to his feet and tackles (B).

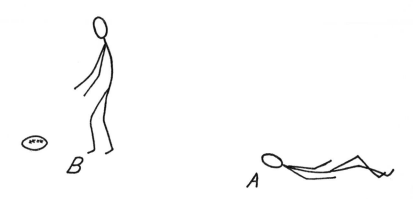

DIAGRAM 5.   Prone Tackling Drill.

f. *Somersault and Hit*

The purpose of this drill is to develop agility, reaction and balance. The somersault places the player off balance and he must reach a position of balance before he can adequately defend or offend.

Player (A) assumes a three-point stance 5 yards in front of (B). Player (A) somersaults and defends himself against (B) who is attempting to block him.

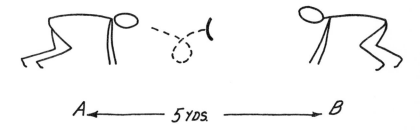

DIAGRAM 6.   Somersault and Hit Drill.

(3) *Strength*—In the game of football there are many of the adjectives that make up the definition of the word strength. Basically, strength is "the power of action in body and limbs." Certainly football requires power and action to a great extent. There is a great need for players of above-average power. To be effective players, they must be able to sustain force without yielding. They must be vigorous and have the strength to endure physical punishment for a lengthy period of time. Stamina derived from physical strength and conditioning has won many football games.

The practical application of strength in a football game requires evaluation of that characteristic by methods that are fairly well identified with the game. After a relatively short conditioning period, the squad should be ready for evaluation to determine their natural strength. This quality is particularly significant in the selection of linemen who must be able to sustain force on every play. Of course, all squad candidates should be encouraged to report for the first practice session in good condition, especially as regards their legs and feet. Then the evaluation drills can be conducted early in the pre-season workouts and at full speed without fear of pulling muscles or creating any serious blister situations.

The 7-man charging sled is a good indicator of strength as is the 2-man sled that is loaded with enough weight (usually an overweight member of the coaching staff!) to make it difficult to move without great effort.

Carrying a weight up an incline will indicate strength. That weight can be in the form of a blocking dummy across the shoulders or a teammate carried piggy-back. Endurance can always be evaluated in this drill by repeat performances with minimum rest periods.

There is no better strength evaluation drill than man-to-man combat. Repeated one-on-one blocking will quickly separate the strong from the weak. Then a natural progression to two-on-one will further point out the strongest players. It is not thought that chin-ups or the lifting of weights are accurate forecasters of the strength required to be an effective football player. Many heavy players are excellent prospects despite their inability to match "chins" with smaller, less heavily muscled candidates. Find the strong candidates, for there is no place in winning football for weakness.

(4) *Size*—This physical asset for a football player is the easiest to measure, and no special instrument other than a scale is required. Care should be taken not to over-estimate the value of size if a player is getting the job done. But there are certain duties on a team that require size, and the big boys who can move are the fundamental building blocks of a successful football program.

In evaluating size and the reading on the scale, obesity should be taken fully into account, for fat serves as a detriment the majority of the time, and firm weight is worth much more to the candidate for the team.

Having evaluated a candidate's characteristics, both tangible and intangible, the coaching staff should now begin to work more closely with the most likely prospects, to determine how quickly they learn football and make progress toward becoming good players. "Coachability" is another factor to be considered for a finer evaluation of the players after the initial squad members have been selected.

Since football is definitely a team sport, and unity of effort means everything to success, the coaches must be certain to spend most of their valuable time with those players who display that they are willing to be a cog in the machinery of the team. The staff must be able to develop the team toward its very best performance. This requirement means that each player must make progress; each player must be "coachable."

Having selected the most skillful, the most apt and the most coachable candidates, the staff should then thrust the athletes into the actual competitive situation of the game they are to play. This means game-like scrimmages. There is nothing better for learning to play the game than actually playing it. The same is true for evaluation of players.

Practicing skills in a limited drill session is beneficial to the development of the player and much easier for the coaches to control; but the final test must be made in game conditions. The controlled drill allows for better teaching techniques in much the same manner as a close-up film scene provides clearer detail than does a wide-angle distant shot. A drill is efficient, too, in that when the coach stops the action to instruct a player, he has a limited number of students to talk to meaningfully. There are not many participants who are not vitally concerned with the point in question. Whereas, in a game condition scrimmage, a halt to the proceedings means dead time for the majority of the players as one man only is being instructed much of the time.

Instruction can best be accomplished for the individual in drills, and the coaches can apply teaching skills more directly in drills; but game scrimmages provide the atmosphere for a more conclusive evaluation of the player's ability and potential as a member of the team. Many coaches have been tremendously enthusiastic about a player who excels in drills only to find, to their dismay, that the same player performs poorly under game conditions. Since the team's record is a result of games and not competition in drills, the coaches are well-advised to withhold final opinion on candidates until after their effectiveness has been fully catalogued in game scrimmages.

Of course, it is more difficult to appraise a single player in a scrimmage because of the greater number of participants and the confused action on every play. The best coaching aid is a film of the action. Motion pictures of a scrimmage do not lie, and player evaluation can be very accurate. Budgetary limitations sometimes prohibits the use of films, but a staff might gain more in the over-all program to film a key practice scrimmage than to film one of the regularly scheduled games. Such tangible evidence of prowess or inability would pay dividends to the staff throughout the season as they could eliminate the poorer prospects and rely more heavily on the better game players. The films should be taken at a pre-set spot on the field, if possible, in order to provide the very best evaluation data. It is recommended that the camera be placed high behind the attacking team, close enough to present excellent detail of the key action. The ball should be returned to the same spot after each play.

Without the great advantage of motion pictures for evaluation of players under game conditions, the coaching staff must take great care to organize their scrimmage sessions. Accurate and complete statistics must be kept for later study. These statistics should include the offensive play number, the key blockers, the ball carrier's individual effectiveness, and the net result of the play with a short remark pinpointing why the play was or was not productive. Defensively, it should be noted who actually made the tackle, assisted, or was within five yards of the ball when the play ended. The net gain should also be recorded.

A student manager can be the recorder, although he should be supervised by a staff member to insure accuracy. The coaches should know the play before the action begins, in order that they can concentrate on a key player or spot along the line. Just as many hunters have learned that a shot into a flock of birds usually misses them all, a coach must not just look at the line or half of the line, but must concentrate his aim on a single player when the action commences. Placing one player under the gun in a scrimmage will speed up the evaluation system. The player under scrutiny should be given a key role on offense for a number of consecutive plays as well as pressured regularly on defense from all angles. He will fail to produce, or establish himself as a game player in very short order.

It can readily be seen from all the factors involved in the evaluation of a football candidate that this is no simple process.

But evaluation of all available players is extremely necessary if a staff is to field its very best. The time spent is worthwhile. Care must be taken for the evaluators to be objective in their analysis. We all have favorite people, and the natural tendency is to make allowances for our favorites. The exact same standards for rating all candidates must be applied, and then, when the final selections are made, the coaches will have put their best players together to form the team that lines up for the kickoff.

3

The Flexible T System

THE AIR FORCE ACADEMY system of offensive football was created to solve a unique problem and to meet the necessary requirement of moving the ball. Every offensive system, of course, has the purpose of moving the ball and eventually outscoring the opposition. Some systems are designed to power the ball by means of a strong, powerful and concentrated ground attack. Others might very well be conceived to move the ball, still on the ground, by means of intricate play patterns based on a great amount of deception. Then there are systems designed primarily to be effective with great emphasis on the pass offense.

The Air Force Integrated Offense Philosophy

In between the extremes of these sound approaches to offensive football, lies the integrated offense, the system that mixes the ground game with the passes in such proportion as to keep the defense honest. It is the integrated offense philosophy that pervades the Air Force Academy Flexible T System.

The unique problem mentioned above which was a determining factor in the creation of this offensive system was the personnel available to play football at the newly-created Air Force Academy. There were very few players (a total of 41 athletes comprised the 1958 squad) and their size and physical strength was definitely limited. So it became apparent that this football

23

squad needed a great number of offensive weapons if it was to
be successful in moving the ball against major opposition. We
were fortunate indeed to have extremely alert athletes who, we
were confident, could absorb a completely new system full of
variations, and make it produce.

And they did just that, as was evidenced by their undefeated
1958 campaign and appearance in the Cotton Bowl at the close
of a great season. The team was dubbed as the "Fabulous Falcons" and certainly contributed an invaluable chapter to the
building of a winning tradition at their brand new school, the
U. S. Air Force Academy.

Natural Skills of the Backfield

The coaching staff spent much of its time, prior to building
the offensive system, in the most important work of evaluating
the natural skills of the available players. It was discovered that
there was an abundance of good pass receivers as well as a
couple of quarterbacks who liked to throw and were adept at the
short pass. It followed that the system should include the pass
offense as a weapon to be used freely.

But our philosophy demands that the ground attack be established before a pass offense can be successful. We believe that
eventually an attacking team must prove it can move the ball
on the ground to be sound and consistent. If we have to prove it
sometime, we might as well prove it to ourselves from the onset.
So, knowing that we could pass, and believing in the pass as an
integral phase of the offense, we set out to create a ground offense
to use as the cornerstone of our offensive system.

The evaluation of the skills of our squad members further indicated that we had some quick-starting inside runners and a pair
of quarterbacks with deft hands and some ball-carrying ability of
their own. These factors indicated to the staff some sort of an
option running series. The regular Split T series was ruled out

because it required mastery at the tackle position to establish the dive-tackle play. So the better ball carriers were to be fullbacks and the main option series adopted was to be the Belly Series. This series would give the ball-carrying chores to the best qualified and would also give the able quarterbacks an opportunity to use their excellent handwork and ball-carrying skill to advantage.

The halfbacks who remained were adequate ball carriers and good pass receivers. They could be used in those roles to balance the "quarterback-fullback" attack that seemed to be the fundamental strength of the ground game. It was thought that the halfbacks could contribute most if employed frequently in strong blocking position; thus the use of wingbacks came into the system. The halfbacks took to the blocking role very quickly and added strength at the major points of contact—the off-tackle holes.

Once set at the normal wingback spot, the halfbacks could block quite efficiently and were in excellent position to run pass patterns. In order to permit them to assume the third role—that is, ball carrier—they were put into motion after the formation had been set. As the halfback started his fly-back motion, he thus placed himself in position to get the ball from the quarterback either by a direct handoff, or a pitch-out from the belly option series.

Making the Most of Linemen's Talents

Having evaluated the abilities of the available backfield men and established a pattern for them, it next became a staff project to make best use of the linemen's skills. What could we ask of the ends, tackles and guards and expect them to contribute to their utmost toward success of the offense? (The center's job was fairly standard and very little time was spent on his particular skills as regards the creation of an offensive system.)

The guards were physically small and they could not be asked to power-block too often. They were not strong enough to blast straight ahead and move out a defender. But they were quick and agile, well-adapted for pulling and leading or trapping. The basic play series, the fullback belly, was aimed off-tackle and outside, so the guards could fire straight ahead or release downfield and contribute to the pattern. Their skills could best be used in pulling out of the line. So a trap series was added wherein the guards were required to pull quickly and trap either the first, second or third defender displaced laterally from them.

As a trapper, they had the key block to perform and they did it well. To their basic pulling role of trapping was added the chores of pulling to lead a sweep and pulling to protect the quarterback on roll-out pass protection or bootleg action. It can be seen from the various pulling roles that the small, quick guards were given responsibilities that they could handle and all the while be contributing to the offensive system.

It has already been pointed out that the personnel were smaller in general than required, and this size problem was particularly significant at the tackle position. A first glance at the available tackles indicated to the staff that the dive-tackle play could not be established as the fundamental play of the system of offense. The tackles could not be expected to control their larger opponents consistently. It was decided, as this conclusion was reached, that both tackles should be aligned side by side to establish one point of physical strength.

As was mentioned as part of our philosophy, sooner or later we would have to move the ball on the ground by brute force (short yardage or on the goal-line) and the requirement of massed strength had to be met. Our solution was to place the two biggest interior linemen next to each other. Thus, the unbalanced line aspect of the Air Force Academy offense came into being.

The two tackles became one unit for power blocking in an

effort to establish one attack point, at least, where our lack of size would not be a real handicap. They were also to be assisted by the wingback in his blocking role.

Since the tackle play dictated an unbalanced line, the staff decided to exploit the advantages of this "old style" alignment as fully as possible. The first move was to establish a left-handedness. The line would be unbalanced to the left primarily in order to place our strength (the double tackle unit) against the opponent's least effective defenders. It had become standard practice to defend against the tendency of most teams to attack to their right. So the indication for us was to pit our strength against the opponent's weaker men. Unbalanced to the left was our beginning.

Because the guards were to be asked to pull out of the line frequently, it was decided to let them stay put on only one side of the center no matter which side of the line was unbalanced. Another consideration was to limit the rules the guards would have to master. As pulling linemen, an element of confusion could have been inserted had the guards been required to play both left and right as were the tackles. The tackles had no pulling duties and the outside, or strong, tackle was always the outside man in the tackle-tandem.

In figuring out how best to employ the ends, there were two main considerations: one end was to be a spread end, or basically a pass receiver, while the other end was to be the short-side end, basically a blocker. The spread end would be given spacing rules so that he could be an effective blocker upon occasion as well as a constant threat as a pass receiver. In view of the fact that the halfbacks were being deployed primarily as wingbacks, the job of spreading out the defense fell upon the long-side end. It was felt that releasing the spread end to run downfield on every play would cause the defense to loosen to cover this potential pass receiver, thus setting up the possibility of an effective long-side running attack.

The emphasis on the long-side offense should have the effect of causing the defense to overshift that way. Such an adjustment would leave the defense vulnerable to the quick thrusts to the short side, especially when the strong-side wingback would employ his fly-back technique to become a potential ball carrier or lead blocker to the short side. Both halfbacks were versed at playing wingback, whether they be on the long or short side of the unbalanced line; therefore the left halfback always plays on his own side, not crossing over as the tackles and ends do.

The Integrated Run and Pass Offense

The great flexibility of the offense became apparent as all of the parts were put together; thus the name given it by the staff— the Flexible T. We have already mentioned some factors that contribute to the flexibility of the offense, all of which are believed to add to its effectiveness, to be extra weapons to fundamental football. Those factors were: unbalanced right and left; spread end (spaced wide and near); wingbacks to long, short, or both sides; and the halfback in motion, or fly-back routine.

All of these factors add to the complexity of an opponent's preparation to defend against the offense. They also give the quarterback many weapons of deployment, running and passing to probe the defense. Additional deployment of the team was made later to further exploit the weapons by use of the slot formation and a flanker set opposite from the spread end.

The staff, following the philosophy of establishing a ground game first, believed that the basic formation, when combined with standard wingback play, provided us with the strength to attack with power. Sometimes this required the spread end to return to a normal position to add mass to the formation. His movement might push the wingback into a normal halfback spot or release the opposite halfback to become the short-side wingback for best blocking position. Just about all of the running game and enough of the passing game could be executed from the massed, or basic, formations to comply with the staff's belief in an integrated run-and-pass offense. In other words, the concentration of forces did not prohibit throwing the ball, but it did increase the power of the attack.

At the other end of the flexibility were the spread formations, which were ideally suited for a passing attack. Enough of the ground game could be run from these deployments to retain the integrated theory of offense. For example, all of the fullback-quarterback attack was intact along with a few halfback plays—at least enough to keep the defense honest when it became necessary or expedient to use the pass as the basic attack weapon.

4

Simplifying the Signal System

The Air Force Signal-Calling System

In ORDER TO USE all of the weapons outlined in the
Flexible T and have them work for you, confuse the enemy and
not your own team.

It is apparent that a relatively simple signal-calling system
must be devised as a vital phase of the offense. As many standard
words as possible should be used as well as a basic numbering
approach. We wanted to stay away from code words or too many
numbers as, when the going gets rough, code words and purely
numerical signals do not always come through clearly to the entire team. Standard terms and a limited number-system tend to
be more understandable even in the heat of battle.

Despite the fact that the attack was to be run from an unbalanced line, the numbering of holes was to remain consistent to
avoid confusion and limit the blocking rules required of linemen.
In other words, a play directed around left end was always to be
identified as a "9" play, whether it went toward the short side or
the long side of the line. Thus a groggy lineman would at least
know that the play was to be aimed toward him or away from
him no matter what formation was called.

The other digit of this simple 2-digit numbering system comes
first and designates the ball carrier: one (1) for the quarterback,
two (2) for the right halfback, three (3) for the fullback and

four (4) for the left halfback. An example of a 2-digit play as called by the quarterback would be "36," which would indicate that the 3 back (fullback) was going to carry the ball at the 6 hole. A further definition to spell out the backfield action or pattern would be to add the series name, such as "belly." So the final play as called would be "36 Belly."

The "Running for Daylight" Approach

It should be pointed out at this time that the second digit of the play number, in this example the 6, merely indicates an attack area and not a specific hole which will be blocked open by the linemen. The fullback should aim at the off-tackle spot, but be fully prepared to run to any daylight that appears as his blockers are moving their opponents through the path of least resistance and not in any specific direction. This technique is all part of the natural way to play football, which is an important aspect of our philosophy of the game.

The only exception to the daylight-running approach is the trap series where execution is geared to split-second timing and the ball carrier must then be disciplined to run exactly on course behind the trapping lineman.

The Descriptive Word in Signal-Calling

It has been explained how the numbering phase of the signal system is used. The addition of a descriptive word brings in another phase of the system. It is believed that everyday words, while completing the mental picture of a play pattern to all players, do not complicate as code words or more numbers might. The word "belly" is certainly descriptive to the team and alerts the fullbacks especially that the quarterback is going to ride along with him with the ball before releasing it to him totally. Another example would be "31 trap." This play is a fullback quick opener straight ahead. The guard is alerted that he must pull and trap at the 1 hole.

Other descriptive terms employed to indicate play series are, for example, power and drive.

Calling the Play Formations

Thus far, the signal system has designated the ball carrier, the point of attack at the line of scrimmage, and the backfield action pattern. The true flexibility of the offense is not found in the various play series, although in the complete picture, a variety of play patterns aimed at the same attack points does add to the number of weapons available to the quarterback. The feature of the offense that makes it the Flexible T is the deployment of the attacking force—the many formations from which the weapons are loosed upon the enemy.

These formations are called in the huddle by descriptive terms, not codes or mere numbers. A mental picture of just how he would like his team deployed is formed by the quarterback, after which he can relay that picture to his team in simple terms. If the quarterback wants his line unbalanced to the left, he simply says, "left." The words "left" and "right" are reserved exclusively for the direction of the unbalanced, or strong, side of the line. This is possible because in the numbering of attack points, or holes, the numbers remain constant and are not aimed at the long or short side.

Thus when the quarterback says "left," the two tackles immediately know that they will be aligned on the left side. The spread end knows he will be to the left and the remaining end realizes that the short side (his domain) will be to the right of center. No other players are concerned with the unbalanced aspect as they position themselves to the same side of center in all formations.

It remains to position the halfbacks in each formation. The

fullback, except as shall be noted later, always lines up directly behind the center and need not be directed to deploy elsewhere. Three basic terms are used to station the halfbacks. The term "double wing" means exactly that, and the halfbacks both set themselves as wingbacks to their respective sides. Their position is basically one foot outside the lineman and one yard off the line of scrimmage. This particular formation, which is used often in the Flexible T, would be called by the quarterback "double wing right." Hearing easily recognizable terms, the line would unbalance right and the halfbacks would both be wings.

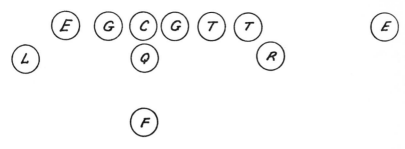

DIAGRAM 7. Double Wing Right Formation.

The term "peel" is reserved for the halfback on the strong side of the unbalanced line. If the line were aligned to the right and the formation called happened to be "peel right," the right halfback would set at the wing spot, while the left halfback would remain at his normal halfback position.

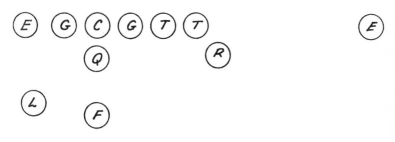

DIAGRAM 8. Peel Right Formation.

The term "flanker" is reserved for the halfback on the short side of the unbalanced line. If the line were aligned to the right and the formation desired were flanker right, the *left* halfback would deploy as a wingback while the right halfback would remain in the normal spot for T formation halfbacks.

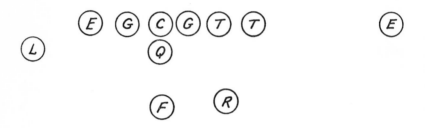

DIAGRAM 9.   Flanker Right Formation.

One extra term which is used as a refinement involves the strong-side halfback and the strong (outside) tackle. It is the term "slot," and adds another pair of formations to the offensive system. When "slot left" is called as the formation, the strong tackle spaces approximately 3 yards from his partner-tackle. This adjustment creates the slot and the halfback on that side stations himself in the center of it.

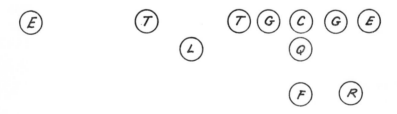

DIAGRAM 10.   Slot Left Formation.

Positioning the Spread End, Flankers, and Fullback

We have described how the quarterback can call eight (8) basic formations (four to each side): double wing, peel, flanker and slot. These formations can easily be varied by further adjustments in lateral position by the spread end, flankers and the fullback.

In assuming a position other than directly behind the center, the fullback applies the principle of putting himself in the most advantageous position to carry out his job on any given play. For instance, if the fullback had to lead the interference on a sweep around left end, he might line up where the left halfback normally would be stationed. He might also move over to a vacated halfback position to execute a pass protection block to that side. Of course, to avoid giving away the play by positioning, he would also move to a halfback spot when not required to do so. The principle of false positioning is also practiced by the spread end and flankers.

The spread end knows where he must position himself on key plays and he makes certain to be there. For example, if the quarterback had called a quick slant-in pass to him, the spread end would take a maximum spacing. Conversely, if the end had a short yardage block to carry out, or had to be downfield to the opposite flat, he would probably line up tight to his tackle. He is also permitted to use all of the multitude of lateral positions in between his maximum (18 yards) and his compact spot. This phase of individual flexibility is gained through constant drilling and applying the general rule, not by any specific spacing assignment on every play. The rule is "to be aligned at the best lateral position to carry out his assignment on any play directed toward him." What he does on the other plays is strictly camouflage to set up the opposition for his key plays. The identical general spacing rule applies to the flanking halfbacks.

The final aspect of flexibility in the offense involves the use of backs in motion, for the fly-back action mentioned before. Once again, this is an individual responsibility and the halfbacks acquire the ability to fly-back on the proper play by constant rehearsal. They do not have to be told to do so by the quarterback. For example, if the formation has placed them as a wingback and the play called assigns them to be lead blockers to the opposite side, the halfback knows he must leave early in order to get into good position to execute his assignment. The same fly-back early would be indicated if an option play had been called to the opposite side, for in this pattern the halfback should be in good position to take a pitch-out from the quarterback.

5

Flexing to Control
the Defense

IT HAD BEEN ASSUMED in the very beginning that
flexibility was a desirable characteristic because it would give the
team an ample supply of offensive weapons, through deployment, as well as play series and the development of fundamental
skills. The multi-formation offense was not designed to accomplish its aims through magic, nor was the entire repertoire intended to be used in any one game. But the weapons were there
to be used as needed. Reasons were always given for deployment
of players, and it was felt that for our type of player the flexibility of varied positioning was beneficial because it has as its
objective the acquisition of effective angles for blocking as well
as massing strength at attack points, besides other key advantages.

Combating the Defensive Corner Linebacker's Strength

Of primary importance is the loosening of the flank defenders
by the deployment of the wide spread end. (It also can be accomplished through spacing the flanking halfback wide to the opposite side.) The most important aspect of this loosening effect
is to neutralize the defensive strength of a corner linebacker.
Ordinarily the corner linebacker can support and defend against

the sweep immediately. His closeness to the line of scrimmage makes him a much more effective defender against the ground game than a halfback. Any deployment, then, should be designed to remove the corner man from his position of immediate support.

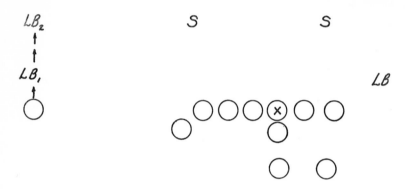

DIAGRAM 11.   Loosening the Corner Linebacker.

The spread end in the Flexible T accomplishes this very nicely as he takes the corner man laterally with him and then pushes him deep as he releases when the ball is snapped. It is believed that the end is spaced too wide to permit the defensive secondary to revolve toward the flow of a sweep run toward the spread end. In other words, the corner man could not release the end to contain the sweep because the safety man on his side would then be responsible for picking up the end as a pass receiver. The distance involved is too great and a simple "flag" route would be disastrous.

One adjustment that was encountered from a corner linebacker (2 deep) defensive secondary was for the wing man or linebacker to loosen and protect deep against the spread end; then when a running play was directed at that point, the deep safety on the side of attack would immediately fill to support the flank. To nullify this defensive move, the spread end's blocking rule was altered to include blocking to the inside on sweeps after starting to push the corner man deep downfield.

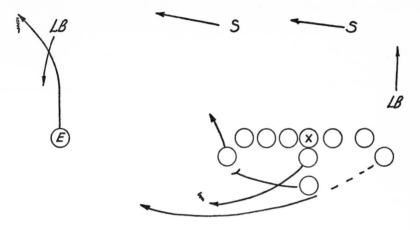

DIAGRAM 12.   Preventing Rotation.

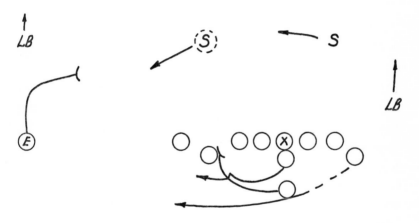

DIAGRAM 13.   End's Role vs. Safety Man Filling.

The first adjustment most corner-type defenses would make when an attack toward a spread end was successful would be to rotate their four-man secondary toward that end. Such a major adjustment would be the same as putting two men on one and would certainly reduce the effectiveness of the spread end attack. However, 2 for 1 is a big price to pay and the resulting weakness to the short side might be readily exploited by the Flexible T.

Using the principle of running and passing away from strength (in this instance quite apparent in the 2-on-1 alignment of the defense) the quarterback would attack away from the spread end with plays aimed at the now-weakened flank.

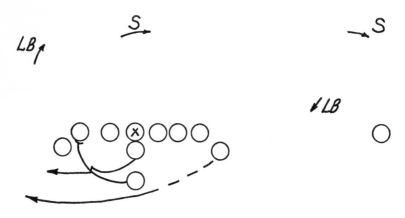

DIAGRAM 14.   Rotated Defensive Backfield.

These effects have been aimed at a corner linebacker type of secondary defense which has the immediate potential of placing nine men into position to defend against the running game. From such a potential, it behooves the offense to deploy in a manner that would weaken the effectiveness. The spread end's lateral spacing has had the same effect as forcing the defense into a position adjustment. In fact, if the corner man covers the end in a man-for-man fashion (something that he usually will do as a result of his isolated position) the deployment serves as a block, for that defender is erased by one offender.

All of these causes and effects that are inherent in the spread end's lateral positioning are also an integral part of the theory of positioning the flanker halfbacks. The flankers are normally placed on the opposite side of the center from the spread end, thus allowing the quarterback the flexibility of attack to either side of his unbalanced line. Setting a wide flanker opposite the spread end also has the effect of making it impossible for the secondary to rotate toward the spread men as there are now two of them.

Of course, many teams employ the three-deep secondary as their basic defense. Such an alignment is quite sound and usually permits eight men to support the ground attack defense immediately, instead of the nine-man potential in a corner-type secondary. The usual advantage is the simplicity of adjustment to spread pass receivers.

The halfback on the side of the spread man normally widens and covers him. Since the halfback had no immediate defensive responsibility as regards the run before adjusting to a spread man, the three-deep adjustment has not particularly weakened the entire defensive picture. However, the spacing of the end has put a big hole in the deep pass coverage as the safety man's zone is tremendously increased and vulnerable to receivers entering it from either side.

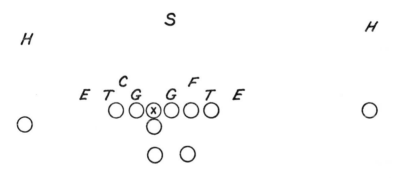

DIAGRAM 15. Spreading the 3-Deep.

The deployment has made it very difficult for the defensive halfback to give any support against a sweep, and thus an additional burden is placed upon the defensive ends as regards containing the ground attack. The absence of a corner linebacker or a quick-supporting halfback lends more strength to an option

play, since the defensive end is somewhat isolated. The unbalanced line aspect of the Flexible T when used against an
eight-man front causes some problems.

The most logical alignment would be to shift the defensive
line over one man to the long side in order to protect that flank
as well as not place the end in a vulnerable position to be
"cracked back" on by a spread end or flanker. But in so doing,
the short side of the defense, without a corner linebacker to help
on the sweeps, is definitely inviting pressure from the offensive
quarterback.

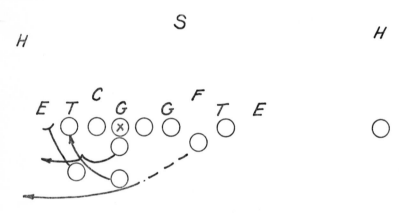

DIAGRAM 16.   Overshifted 6-2 Defense.

This pressure could be exerted by means of a sweep, option
play, quick pitch-out, or a roll out and pressure type of flood pass
pattern.

Role of the Wingbacks

A second advantage in deployment can be gained through the
use of wingbacks. It has been seen how the wings add blocking
power and quick-pass receivers to the attack. They also can
serve the vital purpose of restricting the defensive ends' penetrating into the backfield. Smashing ends can play havoc with a

belly series, but a wingback is in excellent position to turn out on an end and make him think twice before he penetrates recklessly. Such a turn-out blocking assignment also sets the wingback up as the logical man to receive the ball on the screen pass, which is an important phase of the Flexible T pass offense.

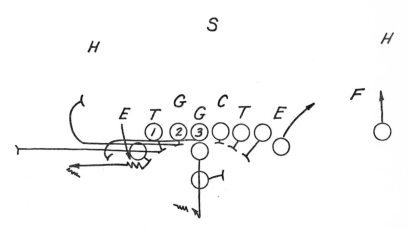

DIAGRAM 17.   Screen Left to Wingback.

Attacking the Slot

A third deployment weapon is the slot and its use is primarily spacing. The objective is to spread the interior defense thin and attack at the slot, using variations of the basic straight blocking. The outside tackle should spread as far as he can and still keep the defensive end on his outside (this usually means a 3-yard slot). Power plays and the fullback slants directed at the slot should pull the defender into the area and set up the outside belly play or the speed sweep or perhaps even cause an over-shifted alignment toward the slot, which will in turn open up the short-side attack.

It has been detailed that the deployment of personnel has added to the flexibility of the offense. Defenders have been made to move laterally to counter a positioning move by ends and

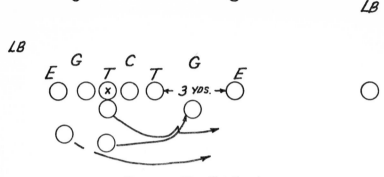

DIAGRAM 18. Slot Spacing.

flankers (or even by the move of the outside tackle, as in the slot). If they have failed to adjust, angles for efficient blocking have been introduced and will be taken advantage of by the offense.

Penetration into the backfield by smashing ends has been discouraged and the pass defense has been spread fairly thin, or forced into a man-for-man situation in certain instances. The inside defenses have been made to adjust laterally because of the linemen's spacing rules and use of the slot between the two tackles, thus becoming vulnerable to quick thrusts or over-adjustment. Therefore, to the many formations, and a few play series, has been added lateral flexibility by the positioning of deployed offensive players.

Timing Variations

Just as a baseball pitcher increases his effectiveness by varying the pace of his pitches from the all-out steam of his fast ball to the medium speed of his curve ball to the teasing slowness of a knuckle ball, so can a football offense be timed for effectiveness.

The baseball pitcher has a favorite pitch, perhaps it's a fast ball, but he cannot depend on that pitch always getting past the batter. Sooner or later the hitter will dig in his cleats, get his eye on that fast ball and knock it over the fence. Many erstwhile big-leaguers have learned this lesson the hard way whenever the established hitters have come to bat against them the second time!

Our belief is that a constant speed attack will permit an opponent on defense to dig in and time his charge and reaction to the pace. This is true whether the offense is attacking quickly (the fast ball), medium (the curve ball), or slowly (the knuckle ball). To add to the effectiveness of the offensive weapons, the factor of timing variations is introduced into the Flexible T.

The three major paces employed complement each other and will greatly improve the yardage gained. For example, the quick reaction required of a defensive lineman to stop the fast pace of a dive play or a quick toss around end, will set him up to be trapped, which is usually a medium-paced play. The lineman reacts immediately to the play action because the quick play has been successful. He must get there right now. But the quarterback has thrown a change of pace at him now in the form of a fake and then a trap block.

This follows the identical principle as the pitcher in baseball who has used his fast ball effectively, but feels that the batter is about ready to knock the cover off his next pitch. So, what does the pitcher do? He eases up, takes some speed off his pitch, and curves the ball, much to the dismay of the batter whose timing is way off because of the change of pace. The result is a strike-out or a weakly hit ball. The same result can be expected in football if the quarterback employs his change of pace after he has set up the opponent's reactions.

The change of pace need not always be from fast to slow, but will be just as effective if applied in the opposite direction. If the slower-hitting plays, such as the long ride of a belly play, the cross-back, second-back-through, the deep reverse, etc., have been used predominantly in the attack, the change of pace indicated would be the fastest one available. In this instance, a dive-tackle play, a quick toss or a quick fullback trap might very well be the play to spring loose a back to go all the way. The defenders might very well be lulled to the slower paced reactions and the "fast ball" play would get by them.

The Flexible T and Change of Pace

The formations from which the Flexible T is run enhance the principle of the change of pace in offensive football. The short side of the unbalanced line provides ample opportunity for the fast attack with the potential of an immediate quick toss, speed sweep or a very rapid option play. The long or unbalanced side of the line provides for the slower pace of the "ride" series and off-tackle power as well as an option play that hits slower. The defensive reactions can be established from the unbalanced line to one side only.

For instance, the quarterback may be setting up the right side as his quick attack and the left (strong side) as his slow-hitting area. Then, after establishing the pattern, the quarterback suddenly shifts his unbalanced line the other way and his left side (short) becomes the quick attack direction. Of course, the short side is not limited to the speed attack only; but it does lend itself well to the change of pace.

The object of flexibility in the offensive system is to control the defense. The opposition has two choices: (1) to adjust to lateral deployment, or, (2) to ignore the spacing and align itself without much concern over spaces between linemen, flankers, wings, slots and spread ends. The Flexible T weapons eventually force the defense to adjust laterally; but this does not preclude the possibility that the defense may not adjust at all or may overadjust. All three reactions can be used to advantage by the Flexible T quarterback.

The defense that refuses to adjust can be attacked with flanking runs and spot passes and will afford the linemen excellent blocking angles to open daylight for the runners. The defense that adjusts laterally will have to obtain its manpower from some other zone that should also be defended, thus creating a soft defensive spot elsewhere, which the quarterback will see and attack with all dispatch. The over-adjusting defense will, of course, present an obviously weak spot somewhere. This situation can best be illustrated by the adjustment wherein two defenders (one close and one deep) cover off with the offensive spread end, who has been effective in catching passes.

Flexible T's Emphasis on Positioning

Positioning is vitally important in all athletic contests, and the Flexible T emphasizes the importance of this principle in football. The "Ted Williams Shift" in baseball was certainly an over-adjustment of the defense in respect to a great hitter. With the entire defensive team aligned heavily toward right field, it became most difficult for Williams to hit safely in that direction. But he had a sure hit if he merely tapped one into left field. The tennis player who fails to regain a central position after each shot can easily be scored against as a major portion of his court would be left unguarded. A boxer who throws a right-hand punch and fails to regain his stance and protective position of his left hand immediately leaves himself wide open for a furious counter-attack. Sound defense requires good positioning. The Flexible T attempts to control the positioning of the defense in order to obtain an advantage for the attack.

6

Developing the Quarterback: The Ground Attack

O UR PROBLEM was a clear-cut one at the Academy, in that we were a new staff, at a new school, and we had a system to install and we had to develop a quarterback with which to run this system.

These remarks are going to be confined completely to offensive quarterbacking, for there are so many different places where coaches play their quarterbacks on defense that it wouldn't be appropriate, in a general discussion, to talk about quarterbacking except from the offensive position. And then, too, you might have the problem we have had upon occasion. The biggest problem with the quarterback on defense is—where are you going to hide him? And this can be bigger than developing him on offense!

Basic Techniques

We believe that there are two basic techniques involved, two basic areas that you must develop with any young boy or any quarterback you are trying to start out with, new, in your system. First of all, of course, is the physical technique that he must use, the mechanics of his footwork and hands in executing his particular assignment on any play. The next part, the one we deem most important, and we will get to that later, is the mental approach.

The physical technique, the mechanics of his position, is covered mostly in spring football. We don't do much in the way of the mental approach to the game in the springtime because we want the quarterback to be mechanically as good as he can be without worrying about the mental approach to any game or how he uses the offense that we have. So let's start off by discussing the physical aspect of becoming a quarterback.

THE PHYSICAL APPROACH

Center Snap

In order to get any play under way with good execution—and this may sound simple, but we can't dwell too much on it—the QB has to get the ball from the center. We work a great deal on this and use a technique which a lot of coaches do, too. It involves the turnover snap, a hard two-handed snap from the center. And we use the two-handed snap mostly because, I feel, it is the easiest to teach, and it becomes most consistent in the shortest time.

We ask the center to put both his hands on the ball and most of the time his strong hand only, the right hand, is just a little bit forward of his weak hand, and we try to rotate the ball so that for a right-handed quarterback the laces are going to come up on his right fingers. We do this with a little adjustment, individually. Our center puts a lot of weight forward, not enough to deflate the ball but he does lean on it, so that he is ready to charge ahead. Most of our offense is run with him popping straight ahead, so we want him to be in an aggressive stance. From a basic position, as illustrated in Plate #1, he snaps the ball up with both hands controlling, rotating it and aiming for a point right behind his cup, with all the pop that he can put into it.

The center's technique is tied closely in with the QB's technique of getting the ball from center. We've had very few mishandles of the ball on the snap from center to quarterback. This is one area that we really believe in, for if you can eliminate this potential error you have the play under way toward a fairly good execution right from the beginning.

QB's Hands

We work a great deal, in the beginning, on the quarterback's getting the ball from the center, using the thumbs together as a basic hand position. Now here, again, there are a lot of ways to do this. We believe that to be consistent and to eliminate errors, using the thumbs-together position, a balanced reception of the ball and a two-handed snap will serve to line up a lot of variables and eliminate some errors. So the QB puts his thumbs on top so they touch the cup of our center.

That is where we start, and then just a little pressure is applied upward. The ball comes up into the hands, so that our quarterback normally gets the ball with a firm grasp when it is snapped. It will come right up there consistently and hard. We like a nice hard snap. A good snap can be heard. The actual sound of a good exchange is "pop." If it's not heard, it's not correct.

After the quarterbacks have been shown by the backfield coaches how to get the ball, we turn this drill between the center and quarterback over to a line coach who works with the two men, paying most attention to the center's technique. We want our quarterbacks to be relaxed and natural. In order for them to be so, they must not be required to make a lot of minor adjustments while they are getting into position to get the ball. We don't want them to worry about that. That is why we have a line coach *getting the center to make all necessary adjustments,* so the quarterback gets the ball *the way he wants it,* based on the fundamental principles of hand-positioning and rotating the ball.

Building Confidence in Center and QB

We constantly conduct drills with only the quarterback and center involved to develop a rapid exchange and to eliminate the potential hazards of ball handling at the outset. The big thing we are trying to build up at this point is a true confidence between the center and the quarterback, so that when a play is called and the snap count is given, the center and the quarterback never have to worry about the ball being put into play properly at the right time. They can think about the other duties they have. The center can think about whom he blocks and how he blocks him. The quarterback can be thinking about how the play is going to develop.

Compatibility

Once we determine which boys are on which team, the center and quarterback on the same unit are going to work together during our practice sessions about 75 per cent of the time. We will rotate them in other drills so that, in the event they do move from one unit to the other, they will be familiar to a certain extent with the pressures, the hand-positioning, and the height of each other so that no big adjustment is necessary. They will be somewhat familiar with each other's technique, but completely familiar with the boy with whom they are going to play in the games.

We feel that this has to be a personal and a very familiar relationship. They have to get the feel of it, so to speak; therefore, we do dwell on this at length. The mastery of ball-exchange technique requires constant rehearsal, and we work on it throughout the spring and fall sessions and every day in our practice warm-ups.

Cadence: Regular Rhythmic Count

The next thing we go to is the emphasis on our cadence—our

count. Here, again, there are a lot of ways of doing this and we have been exposed to just about every variety of count. The object here, too, is to eliminate errors, so that at least the things over which we have control in the game—(1) when the ball is snapped, and (2) how it is snapped—will be executed as well as is possible.

We endorse a regular rhythmic cadence and are going on the same number most of the time. We have change-ups, of course, but we believe that if we know exactly when we are getting off on the ball, and then do it, we have an advantage no matter if the opponent thinks we are always going on that number or not. We are going to eliminate offensive errors because of this. Illegal procedures, people leaning, not knowing exactly when the ball is to be snapped, any motions in the backfield, all are going to be eliminated, or at least reduced to a minimum, by a regular rhythmic cadence. That becomes a part of the players' thinking: they are geared to it.

We use a preliminary command. It serves to "cock" the players in the stand-by-to-go mood. We employ the word "Git," G-i-t. We think it is easiest to say. Even when the QB is out of breath he can say, "Git." And then we proceed, "Git 1, git 2," etc. We "git" into our actual cadence count after having commanded the team to set, and/or adding an automatic check-off. We believe a regular rhythm helps our team to stay on-sides and to get off together when the ball is snapped.

Getting Off Together

A great deal of any offense, and ours is no exception, is based on going straight ahead, and I think the best way to be effective going straight ahead is for the entire eleven to go together. There is not a day passes but that immediately after we have our warm-up (looseners and stretchers), just before we start our drills on the field, for five minutes the squad, in units, does what we call "getting off together."

In this drill we limit our quarterback to running straight-ahead plays with no cross blocking, no pulling linemen; the idea being to explode off the line. We run our basic, simple plays and we have a coach at each end of the line checking alignment and to see that we get seven heads moving together on the snap. We really believe in getting off together and think the snap, the cadence count, and constant repetition are the things that achieve this.

Command Voice Drill

Proceeding with the basic development of the quarterback, we have the ball from center, we have the count. In giving the count, we want the QB's to speak up loud and clear. We hold "command voice" drills. The boys call it choir practice. We get the quarterbacks over in the corner and they all, in unison, bark out the cadence count, the idea being not only to develop their own voice to the extent that they can be heard and their team-mates will perk up and listen, but, also, we want all the quarterbacks to count in the same manner.

Since the count is rhythmic we want our centers and the whole team to get geared to it. All the QB's must say, "Git 1, git 2" at the same level. In this way we attain rhythm and it is consistent with all. The centers get grooved to this manner of hearing the signals and it helps them a great deal to anticipate the snap move.

The Huddle

Command voice has a lot to do with how people receive the orders they are given in the huddle. We want the QB to speak up and take charge. We have an open-faced huddle; the quarterback looks into it and is instructed to get attention merely by flicking his head from the left end all the way over to the right end.

The team's attention is naturally supposed to be glued to him and without any further preparation—this takes about two seconds—he puts out the word on the next play. He tells it loud and clear. We huddle only five yards from the ball, but our quarterback turns his back to the opponent and he speaks as loudly as he wants. We are not afraid that the other team is going to listen. We feel that the vital thing is for our QB to get the message across to his team clearly.

"That Reminds Me of a Story"

One spring, when we started out with quarterback Richie Mayo, who was a freshman at that time, and a freshman at the Air Force Academy doesn't rate very high (they are not allowed to do anything except breathe—and sometimes they are not allowed to do that), he was supposed to be in charge of our football team in the huddle. And this is a difficult thing for a freshman, especially since we had about nine seniors on that team —a pretty tough situation.

As the team came out of the huddle our fullback was a little bit out of position. Richie checked him, looked back and said, "I beg your pardon, Mr. Gallios, would you mind moving over just one step to your left? Would you, please, sir?" And so Steve Gallios, our senior fullback, moved over. But later that fall we had an instance to show how far along a young quarterback can progress as a take-charge player. We came out of the huddle one time in practice and the same thing occurred. Gallios was displaced a little bit in formation and Mayo turned around and we figured, "Here we go again." But instead of saying, "Please, sir, Mr. Gallios," he said, "Hey, Greek, move over."

That's the kind of command development that you want, and a young player grows up in a hurry!

Ball Exchange Drill

The next development stage for a quarterback, once he has the ball from center and he has the count, is to give the ball to somebody else. So we work on the ball exchange to the ball carriers at this stage. The basic drill we use involves just two people.

Prior to the quarterback giving the ball away, the ball receivers have been taught the technique of taking the ball. We use the inside elbow up, forming a pocket, and the carriers are taught to lift the elbow up and not worry about looking for the ball. Just get into position to take it, using inside-elbow-up technique.

Then we put the quarterback and the ball carrier together. Whenever the quarterback is doing anything with the ball, whether it be just practicing getting the count, handing the ball to somebody else, or throwing it, we always get the center to snap it to him. This is the only way he gets the ball in a game and we don't want him to get out of practice or ever lose a chance to get the ball from center in the proper manner. Whether the ball carrier be a fullback or a halfback, we have left and right hand-offs. The quarterback takes the ball and lays it on the ball carrier's belt buckle.

The Natural Way for Quarterbacks

Here, we teach the "natural way." We don't worry about footwork. We want the quarterbacks, who are all built a little differently, to be relaxed and at ease, each one to stand a certain way—his way. We think it is like putting in golf. We have all seen some crazy-looking stances. The same thing applies to quarterbacks as to successful putters. We want them to be comfortable, not worry about where their feet are, how far apart, etc., but just to put their feet any way they feel comfortable. This approach was endorsed by my friend, the great San Francisco quarterback, Frankie Albert.

While I was on duty at my alma mater, Frankie came to Annapolis and worked with our quarterbacks. We really appreciated his approach. His whole idea was, "Be comfortable and be natural and the rest of the pattern is going to fall into line," so we don't worry about where our feet are, unless the boy is ineffectual. If he is not getting the job done, is awkward and is holding up the rest of the backs because of it, then we will work with him on special placing of his feet and balance; but otherwise we want him to be completely natural.

Security in Ball Exchange

We emphasize the "soft and sure" placing of the ball to the man who is going to run with it. *The responsibility for the ball exchange is on the quarterback.* The ball carrier just makes a pocket and runs to his spot. Most of the time if we are going straight back, the ball is handled in two hands for a surer placement; but on our dive plays, quick slants or any other play where quickness is involved, we normally like to reach the ball to the ball carrier. Then it will be a one-handed exchange.

Normally, the boy is going to keep his strong hand on the ball. I say "strong hand" because we have had left-handed quarterbacks and they are allowed to use either hand. But normally, a right-hander would keep his right hand on the ball. He can reach further with one hand than he can with two because he can twist his body. The QB gets the ball with two hands, but ends up with just one in control.

And we don't like the quarterback to slap the ball into the ball carrier. There is no fake involved in such a move. It is just a matter of ball exchange, so if the QB is not faking, why not look at the spot where he is going to put the ball and put it in there nicely, softly, causing no problem for his own teammate?

The QB takes the ball and aims for the belt buckle and lays

it in there. He doesn't throw it, he doesn't slap it, he doesn't pop it in there. He puts the ball straight out and lays it on the buckle, in the pocket. The quarterback doesn't release the ball until he is sure of the exchange. It is his responsibility.

To insure execution, the quarterback must not be looking up in the air or out in left field somewhere as if there is a big fake involved. He merely looks where he is going to put the ball. The pattern makes the fake.

Combat Conditions

Then, after this ordinary hand-off drill, we go to the drill that Bud Wilkinson made famous. We call it the Oklahoma drill. It involves a live hand-off drill with a defensive man between two blocking dummies, an offensive blocker, a ball carrier and the quarterback.

The quarterback now gets a little closer to actual combat conditions. He has to take the ball and hand it off with people knocking into each other all around him. We work this drill a lot. We think it is one of the best drills in football. It involves so many basically sound principles, ball handling, blocking, tackling, running to daylight, all the contact that goes on around a ball exchange in a football game.

Play Patterns: Quick Hand-off to "First Man Thru"

The next thing we do in the development of the quarterback is to put in a play pattern involving an entire backfield. One of our basic simple plays is used to stress timing—the timing is vitally important. The quarterback must get the ball to the man who is going to run with it, *at the right time.* And then, on certain plays, like a fullback trap, or our inside drive, we drill with just two men.

For instance, on the fullback trap, or any quick trap play, we like to work with just two men so that we don't complicate it.

And here, again, we are trying to foster confidence—the same reason why we always work the QB's together with the centers. We are trying to produce confidence so that the ball exchange and the quick timing of the play isn't a touchy mental factor to the players when the signal is called in a game.

With a real quick, fast-timing play like the FB trap there is no fake involved. We merely ask the quarterback to open up and put the ball out at the right level, and the fullback knows it is going to be there, and can pick it off. We walk through it, and then we run through it at half speed, then we go full speed, and pretty soon we have the necessary confidence. The fullback knows the ball is going to be there; the quarterback knows he doesn't have to take it back to him; he is going to open up, hold out the ball and the fullback will take it.

Once we have the fullback and the quarterback confident that the ball exchange is going to be good in the quick trap series, the next step is to get the fullback to follow the pulling guard. This is included in the same area of confidence. That fullback knows he can go full speed: he is sure to get the ball, the guard is going to be out of his way, and they all go full speed. In a play

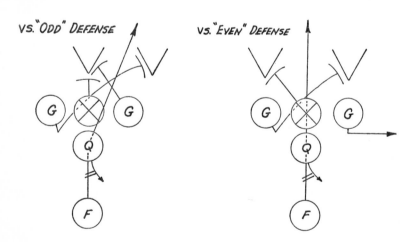

DIAGRAM 19.   QB-FB Trap Drill.

like this, it is a four-man drill: quarterback, fullback, guard and center.

Fake and Give Drill

Next comes another two-man drill, which again involves the fullback. This drill is leading up to a quarterback technique which is used in many offensive patterns: *faking to the first man through and giving to the second.* It involves the fullback's driving hard over guard. Here, again, there is a little special technique, a delicate timing between two people, and we want this to be a confident move.

In the inside belly or drive series, we want that fullback to know he can run full speed very close to that quarterback and do a more than adequate job of faking without doing anything else except running real hard, low and fast, lowering his inside shoulder. That is all the fake we want from him, and we want that shoulder down because it is going to hide the ball and also is going to be ready to blast somebody we'd like him to block. Here, again, we work strictly on the quarterback getting that ball and opening straight back. He has the ball with both hands. He is not going to give it to the first man through, and the only fake we want is movement of the quarterback and the fullback converging on a point. We want both hands on the ball because the quarterback wants to be certain to hang on to it until the fullback gets by and the next man comes.

The fullbacks know how close they can run to the quarterback, not getting in the way, and doing an effective job, so we work them hard on this series with just two men prior to adding the third man, the halfback who carries the ball.

The coaching technique that we think to be very important at this stage in the development of the quarterback has to do with the various heights and postures of the backs he works with in sets.

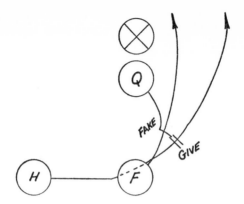

DIAGRAM 20.   2nd-Man-Through Drill.

If you have two normal-sized people, the quarterback and the fullback both about the same size, there is no problem—each player in a slight crouch, and the ball is at the right level. But if you have one quarterback who is 6′3″ and one fullback who is 5′9″, the disparity in their heights would cause a problem. Here, again, that is why we like the QB's to drill mostly with the people with whom they are going to play in the game. You should change sets about one time out of four, so that they will work with others with whom they may have to play. A tall boy at quarterback giving that ball, or faking through a series with a short fullback, is going to create a problem unless he adjusts for it. The short player can't do much about it, but the tall player has to come down to his level.

The Option Play

About the only live contact drill to which we expose our quarterbacks involves the option play. We run our option mostly off the belly series, and in the spring sessions we teach quick, decisive moves for the QB. We want the QB to have an option, true, but it is a clear-cut one. In other words, the quarterback comes out to option spot and he either turns the corner and runs with the ball or else he pitches it off. We start out by giving the QB a clear-cut picture of the option where there is only one move that is the right one. Diagram #21 shows just what our option series drill looks like.

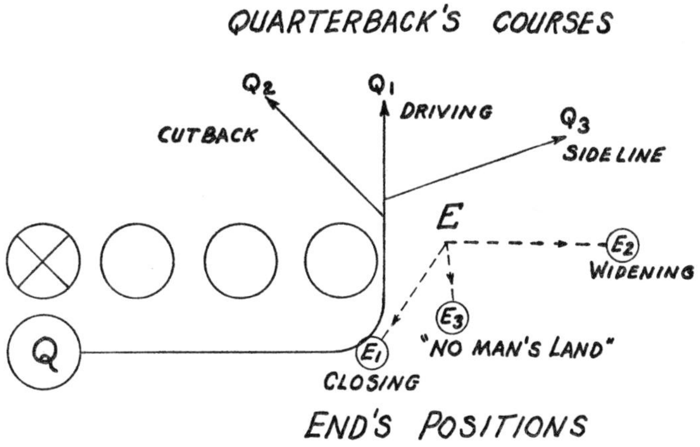

QUARTERBACK'S COURSES

END'S POSITIONS

DIAGRAM 21. Quarterback Option Drill.

We put a defender at end and we walk through this to show the quarterback the two basic positions that the end can assume. If the end is in position #1 and is closing, the quarterback should pitch out. If the end is at position #2 and then widens right away, the quarterback should keep and cut up the field. When the QB keeps, the basic move is to cut right now. And when he cuts he has three routes to take:

1. Run a course at right angles to the line of scrimmage, driving for yardage (as on the goal line or when a first down is imminent).

2. Once past the scrimmage line, break at 45° back against the flow.

3. Break at 45° or flatten toward the sidelines (with the flow).

Of course, there is another option set up if the QB breaks
to the sidelines, but some boys are more effective running
against the grain. If they are, we want them to cut back as they
might break for a pretty good gain.

Once the QB understands the options the defender has
given him, we walk through the variations that he may encounter. It is simply a matter of recognition as to what the
defender does. Then we run through it, making sure that the
man on defense is doing one of the two basic moves and nothing
else. He either comes right now or he widens right now, so that
the quarterback will recognize an obvious situation, one or two,
cut up, or pitch out.

Make a Definite Move

The next thing we do is throw in the factor that happens
mostly in the games. [Reference Diagram 21, move to position
E or position E2; but rather plays in what we call "No Man's
Land." (E3).] When he does that, he sort of holds his ground.
Then we stress that the quarterback, who has the ball, has to
make a decisive move. We don't want it to be a guessing game;
we don't want him to be trying to fool anybody now. But we
feel that a decisive move is called for, even though the defender
is not in the right spot for us to do one or the other. So, when
the QB comes out on the option in our live drill, the defender
is now either in one, two, or a third position, which is "No Man's
Land."

We still want the quarterback to make a quick, decisive
move. He comes out and normally, if the defender is in "No
Man's Land," the quarterback uses the "freeze" move. In other
words, he will come out and if he is a quarterback who prefers
to run with the ball—and there are some like this—he crisply
fakes a pitch and cuts up right now. The idea is to freeze the
defender in "No Man's Land" with a quick fake.

If the QB prefers to pitch out, he comes out to the defender in "No Man's Land," quickly fakes to cut up and then pitches out. It's like a head fake in basketball. The same principle is used. We want a decisive move. We don't want the option to drag on out until the pursuit comes over and ruins the play.

This live drill spells out the option play and it stresses deliberate moves. We don't want the QB fooling around; we want him to do something positive. We always teach that if you are going to make a mistake, make a good one, make one that can be recognized. That means that you did something real wrong or real right. That is the way we approach the option play for the QB's.

The teaching of the live option drill wraps up the mechanics of developing a QB in the area of the ground offense. We have taken him through these steps:

1. Stance.
2. Technique of getting ball from center.
3. Cadence count.
4. Ball exchange.
5. Faking to first man and giving to second.
6. Running the option.

7

Developing the Quarterback:
The Passing Attack

As REGARDS PASSING, our quarterbacks are assigned about 95 per cent of the forward passing, so they
practice it a great deal. We throw about 25 passes a game and,
since that is about one-third of our offense, we think we ought
to spend just about that proportion of time on it in our practice
sessions. We believe in throwing the ball and like to integrate
it with the running game.

The physical technique of passing is important to us. Of
course, it is nice to have a quarterback who can pass. It is a real
tough coaching job to teach a boy to throw the ball if he can't
throw naturally. We don't want to leave you with the impression that we take a quarterback who can't throw and make a
passer out of him, because we don't. We prefer to stress the
natural way. If the player is a side-armer, but he throws the
ball well, we don't change his motion. If the boy is having
trouble, if his natural motion is not a real good one, we may
try to change it a little bit; but if he can throw the ball, using
his natural motion, that is what we want.

DEVELOPING A PASSER

We have had underclassmen who had potential, but had
some mechanical things wrong with their throwing motion. We

work with them, because they have the potential but are ineffectual the way they are.

Mostly, there are three things we think can be done for this type of passer:

1. Footwork
2. Balance
3. The grip on the ball

From the footwork standpoint, we feel that when a passer throws the ball, he must have his feet in the right position or he will be throwing across his body—off balance. Unless he is real strong, throwing off-balance is a most difficult thing to do. Work on footwork, it's the key to accuracy in forward passing.

Footwork: Stepping in the Throwing Direction

We throw a lot of sideline passes and break-out patterns. In throwing across his body a passer has a tendency to underthrow, which is fatal. If he is going to throw to the right he must step that way. It is tough to throw any other way because he is throwing all with his back and arm and not getting his legs into it. We work on the footwork of stepping in the direction that you are throwing. We stress footwork, using our leading foot as the pointer to where we are going to throw.

Some boys don't do this naturally, but when we are throwing timing passes, which is our basic approach to pass-offense, footwork is very important. Richey Mayo, our passer, was a natural at this sort of thing. There was nothing we had to do with his footwork. He had good balance and threw the ball well.

Completing the Pass

The result we want, like anybody else, is the forward pass that is completed to somebody on our team, and we don't care whether or not the ball spirals. Of course, it photographs real well if it spirals, but we just want the pass to be completed.

Our alternate QB, John Kuenzel, threw a "knuckle ball." The ball floated and wobbled, but we caught about 58 per cent of the ones he threw, so we didn't mind that it was a wobbler. Pepper Rodgers, our QB Coach, played a lot of football for Georgia Tech and he was a "wobbly" passer, but he completed sixteen in the first half of the Sugar Bowl Game one time. They all wobbled. They all were completed. So we don't care if it doesn't spiral; just get it to your teammate.

Timing the Pass

The timing mentioned is the basic fundamental of our pass offense. We throw timing passes. Why?

At one time, at the Naval Academy, we were coaching the defensive backfield and couldn't have been more impressed with any single thing in football than a well-timed pass. We couldn't stop them. So consequently, we came to believe in timing, no matter whether passing from straight back, rolling out or passing after a play action in the backfield. We throw the ball at a specific time. We believe that this can be done whether you are throwing a 2-yard pass or a 50-yard pass. You can change the elevation from a bullet to a nose-up, punt-type pass and still get it off at the same time and work anywhere from two to fifty yards on the same timing.

Throw It NOW!

The pass is thrown at the right time to our No. 1 pattern man. If he is covered at that time and we can't release the ball, we quickly look for our safety valve. We have a secondary receiver who is in the pattern; but if he is not open, we run with the ball or throw it away. This holds true unless there is an emergency and we must complete a pass to retain possession or score a touchdown. (Example: Last minute of the half or near the end of the game when a desperation completion is required.)

We would prefer not to "read" the entire pattern, searching for that one man who is open. We don't want the quarterback to be running around back there and looking for somebody to throw it to, having made up his mind beforehand that he is going to throw the ball, no matter what. Timing! Throw it now. If not, safety valve; if not, run; try to get back to the line of scrimmage.

Selecting the Receiver

We work closely with the receivers on pass patterns to determine their skills. The quarterbacks have to be familiar with the individual abilities of the pass receivers as well as all the patterns. We teach the passer to throw to the dependable receivers.

For instance, when a clutch play comes up there is always one player on the team who will be most likely to catch the ball. We sell it to the QB this way: "It's going to help your pass completion record if you throw it to the man who will catch it." It isn't hard to sell when you do it that way—all passers are proud of their completion record. The QB might now and then otherwise try to spread it around and throw to this fellow, that fellow, and the next one.

Throw to the player who is sure to catch it. After all, that is what we want to do—complete the pass.

Screen Passes

One of the weapons we spend a lot of time on in our pass offense is screening. We screen a lot and believe in the screen pass. It is a fine weapon, especially to counter-balance the basic pass offense. The screen is a mandatory part of the passing game. A lot of practice is allocated to the screen, and timing is vital. We rehearse the line by themselves as a three-man screen of blockers. They learn their assignments prior to being co-ordinated with the backs. No. 1 man is a lead blocker, No. 2 man a personal interferer, and No. 3 man a block back.

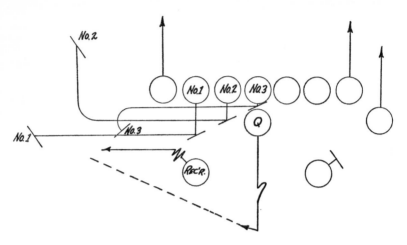

DIAGRAM 22.   Screen Technique.

Screen Technique

In a normal three-man screen the QB drops back and sets, then the No. 1 man of the screen will lead and block out on the signal, which is normally after a two or three count, and the No. 2 man will be personal interferer for the ball carrier, No. 3 man will block back. We have seen so many screens that looked like they were going to go all the way with three people out in front, and all three took the same man, or all three missed the same man. To avoid this, we give the screening linemen definite assignments. No. 1 blocks out, No. 2 leads, No. 3 blocks back for an opponent who "smells" the screen and attempts to catch it from behind.

The next phase of this screening is to use an audible signal. Since we vary from a two-count screen to about a four- or five-count screen, the quarterback, as he goes through his act—and that is exactly what it is, an acting performance—says, "Go," when he is ready to release the ball. We want our men to know exactly when they can move out as a screen and take off at full speed.

We throw lead-pass screens. We don't have our receivers set up as stationary targets. The receiver hits, slides, and then runs for the sidelines. We throw him a lead pass, so in the event he is covered, the ball can be thrown out of bounds. Or in the event the opponent is right with him, he can run away from him.

Just about every day we have a screen drill. The line and the backs are separated at the start. Then we bring them together for a little dummy work. The screen pass is a special technique and you have to work a long time with your quarterbacks until they get to be good actors. It is a big act and must be rehearsed often against all varieties of defensive moves and pressure.

QB'S THREE PASSING TECHNIQUES

There are three types of passing techniques that a QB must master:

1. Drop-back or cup
2. Roll-out
3. Play-action or bootleg

All three are important in the complete pass offense and are naturally most effective when used at the correct time during a game.

Drop-Back Pass

In executing the drop-back type of pass, the QB must understand that his protectors are forming a cup and guarding a spot.

If the QB is to take full advantage of the security offered by a cup, he must throw the ball from the protected spot. We believe that he should normally move quickly back to a depth slightly deeper than the spot, and then step forward as he

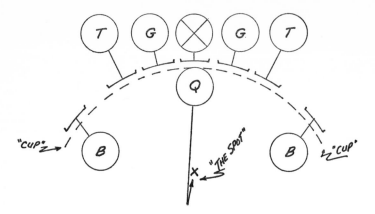

DIAGRAM 23.   Cup Pass Protection.

passes. He will then end up on the spot and be fully protected.
Constant drills will develop his confidence in the teammates
who are guarding him and his spot. We recommend that the spot
be 6 yards directly behind the center.

Roll-Out Pass

The roll-out style of passing offers less positive protection
to the QB, but affords him:

1) The opportunity to run away from the overloaded rush,
   and,
2) Pressure on the defensive flanks with the threat of a fake
   pass and run.

The protection now tends more toward an area rather than
a spot as in the cup. The QB must be prepared to run to avoid
rushers and must also be ready to pass on the move if the
receivers are open. The QB must stay relaxed and mobile in
order to be effective as a roll-out passer.

Play-Action or Bootleg Pass

Just as with the screen technique, the play-action pass re-

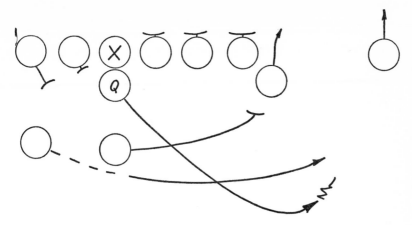

DIAGRAM 24. Roll Out Technique.

quires a bit of acting on the part of the QB. He must pretend that the ball has been handed off to another back after the team has executed what appears to be a running play. The time thus consumed, and the faking employed, have permitted one or more receivers to break clear downfield, and a pass play develops. The very word "bootleg" indicates a stealthy move and

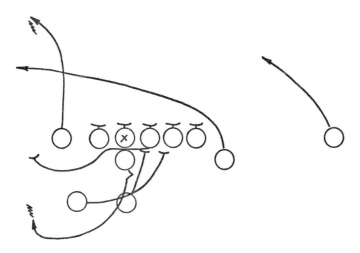

DIAGRAM 25. Bootleg Pass.

that's exactly what takes place as the QB, with iron nerves, nonchalantly holding the ball on his hip, turns his back to the opposition (much in the manner of a bullfighter) and then throws a pass at exactly the correct moment.

The bootleg technique affords the QB minimum protection and must be called when the defense is least suspecting a pass. The faking and timing mean everything. Ham it up!

8

The Mental Approach
to Quarterback Strategy

H AVING COVERED the physical techniques in the
development of a quarterback, we now proceed to the most
important phase in his development: strategy, the mental approach. After all, the QB is a player who has to do the thinking
for the coach on the field. He has to give the orders. He has to
do the majority of the intellectual work of football while the
game is going on. Thus we believe the mental approach, the
technique used in developing the quarterback mentally, is the
most important area of all.

KNOW THE OFFENSE

Even with a complete offense and with some fine football
players, all will be ineffective unless they are employed at the
right time and place. During the game the plays and players
must be used efficiently. If a coach is to be of service to the
quarterback during the game, the quarterback has to think
somewhat the way he does, and he has to thoroughly understand the offense. So we tell our QB's how our offense was
planned, how it was put together and why. We do that in lec-
tures with them, and any other time we get a chance: on the
field, before practice or after practice, in the training room,

we like to talk to them about the why-and-wherefore of the offense.

Timing and Rhythm

Timing is a vital fundamental in our offense, not only in passes, but in runs. We have a three-phase timing plan for our runs. We have:

1) Quick Timing in our trap series and the straight-ahead plays.
2) Medium Timing, which is normally the second-back-through the line. The QB fakes to one and gives to another, either counter or with the flow.
3) Slow Timing, which has to do with reverses, draw plays and slow fake plays like the belly series.

. . . One, two, three phase-timing.

This aspect of our offense is explained to the QB using the example of a big-league pitcher whose best pitch is:

1) The fast ball. Then when the batter digs in for that blazer, he is thrown
2) A medium speed curve ball. Finally to round out his repertoire the pitcher has a real fooler,
3) A knuckle ball.

The batters would have a picnic if he threw at only one speed all day.

We believe that the offense must be a complete one, and we feel we must have all the basic offensive weapons (running plays and pass patterns) that we need to play any football game right from the beginning of the season. Put the offense in for the squad as a complete package. The QB then has a repertoire to call upon as needed.

Any changes that we make during the season are only alterations or changes in the sets. We put the wing here instead of there, or put him in motion, or we flop over right-handed instead of left-handed. We never change the whole offense.

MAKING EVERY PLAY COUNT

In the very beginning we emphasize to the quarterback that our objective in any game is to *eliminate the wasted plays.* Those plays that apparently won't go so well in a given game, because of the particular defensive alignment, we want to eliminate from our basic offense.

The quarterbacks are told how every play in a series is constructed, why it should work, and the defensive alignments or tactics that may be used against us that would render it less efficient than it was designed to be. We spend a lot of time on the field with the quarterbacks and backfields in groups, developing a series of plays, putting the companion plays with the basics and the passes that go with them and trying to show the quarterback how these things fit together and how they should be used. Also, how and when they should *not* be used.

QB's Knowledge of Defense

Before a quarterback can use the complete offense objectively, he has to understand defensive football. This chapter concerns the QB on offense; but we believe he must understand defensive football first. In order to do that, we try to impart a basic knowledge of defensive football to our quarterbacks, teaching them the aspects that are strongest and weakest in a particular defense. We don't discuss personnel within a defensive pattern because we are merely teaching the general principles of defense, not personalities.

Perimeter Play

We teach the fundamentals of backfield rotation, adjustments to flankers and spreads and the different basic types of pass defense that teams use. We try to give the quarterback a general knowledge of what adjustment problems he causes the defense as he deploys his team. The QB must know the way the defense lines up, with the understanding that there is no one defense that solves all the problems. Each defense has strengths and weaknesses, and he must understand them if he is to attack them intelligently.

We do this in four ways:

(1) We lecture our QB's with the aid of a blackboard.

(2) We run film clips or highlights of a certain defense, showing where it is most difficult to run or pass against.

(3) Then we walk through plays out on the field. We line up players wearing different-colored shirts and walk through different perimeter adjustments, loosening a corner man here or rotating a whole backfield behind him, or playing the three deep and the different styles of end play. The strengths and weaknesses of all the adjustments are thoroughly covered. These sessions are involved with only the perimeter people, the ends and the backs, and what they can do to hurt you.

(4) We scrimmage against various defensive alignments. We want our quarterbacks to be most knowledgeable about perimeter people; and then, in half-line scrimmages we cover what the interior linemen do.

Since our offensive deployment will not cause much in the way of adjustment in the middle of any line, we should understand most what the perimeter people do. We scrimmage our basic plays against only one defense. For instance, in one drill period we show the quarterbacks the best plays to attack this particular defense, and the plays to stay away from because they will be wasted. Do not attack the strength of any defense as a starting point—probe the weaknesses.

QB Must Know His Teammates

When our offense is fairly well understood and the basic knowledge of defenses and adjustments have been mastered, we feel we can prepare a particular game battle plan if we add to this a thorough knowledge of what our own players can and can't do.

We objectively talk to our quarterbacks about their teammates' abilities, in order not to appear partial, and we ask them to evaluate their own teammates honestly. We want the quarterback to know who is the best blocker, who is the best short-yardage runner, who is the best man to throw the ball to in a clutch. This can be the least bit difficult because the QB has some friends on the squad who are closer than others; but we sell it man-to-man that football is a tough world. He must pick the right man at the right time and he must understand who can and who cannot. He gives the ball to the best ball carrier and you put him over the best blocker and you get the job done, personalities excepted!

PREPARING FOR AN OPPONENT

Quarterback strategy, meaning preparation for any single game, can be developed after the QB's fundamental skills, and after all information about his own offense and team has been acquired.

In preparing for an opponent, we like to deal in generalities when we talk to our quarterbacks. We don't want them to be all cluttered up with details. The scouts and our film review give the staff a sufficient lot of detailed information. It is our job to boil this down to the essentials, and this is what we give our quarterbacks. Normally, we do this at our scouting meeting and we also have lunch with the quarterbacks twice a week and talk about the general characteristics of our opponent.

How Good Are They?

The first important point we want to get straight with the QB is whether or not the opponent is stronger than we are—are they a better team? If the answer is yes, we then decide what degree of gambling will be involved in our approach to the game. If they are better than we are, we have to gamble to beat them. If they are not as good as we are, we can play a little closer to the vest. If they are a lot better than we are, we really have to unload and simply turn loose with every weapon we have.

So we give the quarterback a general impact and it must be an honest one, as honest as we can make it. We do not believe in telling him that our rival is as good as the Chicago Bears and it's a shame we have to play them, if that team really is no better than we are. We tell them. We don't use this same approach with all of the other men on the team; but our quarterbacks know—and they must—man to man, what our chances are against each team we play.

What Kind of Team Are They?

Secondly, we want a determination of the "personality" of our opponent. Personality is a unique word to apply to a football team, but it fits. We mean their style, their offensive and defensive manner, and their tendencies during any game.

We chart our scouting reports so that we know what their play selection tendencies are for sidelines, short yardage, long yardage, time in the game, etc. All of these factors added together equal the opponent's personality. We describe to the quarterbacks the personality that has been derived from all this information. For example: a team may have a personality like some men do—conservative, cautious, orthodox. Or another might be flamboyant, aggressive and reckless. One might be a fancy boxer, another a slugger. There are all kinds of teams, just as there are all kinds of men.

Who's Who?

Finally, we give them some general information about the personnel. We are not great for details as regards scouting the opponent's personnel. We don't say that "when this guard puts his right foot back he pulls to the right," or that "when this tackle grunts twice it means he is going to post block." We tell the team who the better football players are—who to avoid. We don't pass along details that would detract from the general approach to a football team. We don't have the time.

The Actual Battle Plan

A battle plan is made and the quarterbacks are brought into its creation. We ask them what they think we should do. We have our own ideas, and if the QB's don't agree completely with us, we listen. We have a master list of all our plays and series. It is a big, long, and complete list. Normally, we take the general battle plan and use it as a guide to prepare for each game.

Each week we red-line all the plays that we don't believe are going to make it in this game—that usually makes a lot of red lines. From this master list we eliminate the plays we have classified "inefficient" and then outline our choice, based on the staff's work and the QB's ideas. We retain the "bread and butter" plays all the time, and we stress that the QB should always employ to the utmost the teammate who is having a good day. Just as when a basketball player gets hot, give him the ball and let him shoot.

At the Game: Getting Started

On the day of the game we actually tell the QB the opening series of plays to call. We don't want him to be worried about anything at that stage. This relieves him of an unnecessarily immediate responsibility and gives him the opportunity to ease into the game as an individual player. We usually try to have everybody just run into somebody on the first play (a wedge) in order to relieve their tension.

We believe that at the half-time we should alter our plan a bit by further elimination of the inefficient plays which have not panned out so well. We believe that our biggest enemy in any football game is having too much offense and not enough time to use it in. The quarterback may often feel he has to use it just because we practiced it during the week. So we eliminate more of the plays at the half-time.

We always brief our quarterbacks, when they are on the bench, concerning the latest adjustments in the game, which have been picked up by the spotters. And once in a while we send in a play (but only when it seems sure to be effective!).

THE QB's MATURING PROCESS

In the case of Richie Mayo (as regards the development of a quarterback), a sophomore who had never played QB in a college game, he didn't start in a game for the first half of the season. He played about 40 per cent of the time, but he never started. We didn't think it would be expedient to put that pressure on him. We figured it might be a little too much for him. And then, about the middle third of the season, we put him in to start the second half of a game. The last five games on the schedule, he started every game. That was the way he was brought into the game atmosphere, without a great load of responsibility being loaded abruptly on his shoulders.

Another reason for easing a young QB into the game pressure is to relieve him of the task of probing the defenses to find out the most efficient plays. That should be done for him. Johnny Kuenzel, our alternate QB, did that for Mayo, and what a fine job he did! When Mayo went into the game, he had a pocket full of weapons and was able to go full speed. That brought him along a lot faster than otherwise might have been the case. He acquired confidence in a hurry.

There are many ways of developing a quarterback; this is just the way it happened with us at the Air Force Academy.

Strategy development is vitally important. We believe strongly in timing and in prompt elimination of the inefficient. We like to expand on this aspect most with our quarterbacks: (1) the mental approach, (2) getting to know us, (3) our system, and (4) "why" we do things. We prefer a close personal relationship between the QB and the coach during the games. The only way to get this is to have a personal relationship with the quarterback year 'round. Get to know him and talk with him. Whenever we have a chance, we have lunch with the quarterbacks, or try to have them stop by the office so we get to know each other. Then on Saturday afternoons they are going to make us real proud.

9

The Longside
Fullback Belly Play

THE DOUBLE WING T belly series has provided the "bread and butter" plays of the Flexible T offense. The main weapon in the series has been the fullback hitting at the off-tackle area. The fullback off-tackle play establishes the series and is run more often than any other single play. As will be clarified later, the off-tackle play is not precisely that, but it is basically a daylight run that is aimed at a point inside the defensive end.

THE FULLBACK BELLY PLAY (36 BELLY)

This play has been the basis of our running attack. It is believed that the defensive team cannot adequately defend this off-tackle play and the companion outside belly option play by the use of only one defensive alignment, technique or coverage. Although this play seldom breaks away for the extremely long gainer, it adds a consistency that provides a solid building block for a fundamentally sound ground attack. Consistency in this instance indicates that a play gains 3½ yards or more per attempt, thus providing continued possession of the ball for the offensive team.

The first year that the fullback belly play was used, it

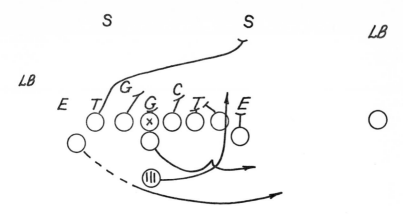

DIAGRAM 26.   Longside Fullback Belly Play.

averaged slightly over 5 yards per attempt, and was 80% consistent or successful. This play filled a major role in the Falcons' undefeated Cotton Bowl season of 1958, the year the Air Force Academy had its very first senior class.

Naturally, the fullback belly play is dependent upon the outside belly option play for much of its success. The defense normally will guarantee the flanks and be slow to effect any drastic adjustments in halting the constant thrusts of the off-tackle play. In accordance with our basic theory of not trying to run an inefficient play, we would be quite satisfied to rest the fullback belly should it be well defended. However, in stopping the fullback belly, the opponent normally would leave itself wide open to the outside belly option play, which would automatically become the prime weapon with the fullback off-tackle given a secondary role.

The 36 Belly Run Shortside and Longside

Since the Flexible T offense runs from an unbalanced line, the fullback belly play as executed to the long side differs from the same play when directed to the short side. The reasons for this difference are twofold.

First, the point of attack at the line of scrimmage is *wider* to the long side, which forces the fullback to run a different course if he is to be in position to hit the line at a right angle. This perpendicular attack course is stressed because a right angle at the line of scrimmage enables the fullback to cut left or right as well as continue on course straight ahead, wherever the daylight should appear. When directed to the short side, the fullback belly play is aimed at a point of attack over the short-side end, or just two linemen removed from the center.

The point of attack to the long side is outside the second lineman, and since the fullback belly play is usually run from a slot formation, it is aimed at the third man removed from center.

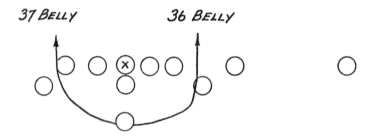

DIAGRAM 27.   Attack Points for Fullback Belly.

In order to hit the attack point at the perpendicular angle as mentioned above, the fullback must vary his course from the more direct slant to the short side. The second difference between the longside and shortside fullback play is a result of this difference in course and involves the *timing* of the play. The shortside play retains the basic shortside timing of the un-balanced T attack; it is a quick-hitting play. The fullback runs at full speed and the quarterback must move at top speed to transfer the ball to him in a direct hand-off.

The longside fullback belly play, on the other hand, is a relatively slow play as the fullback moves laterally and under control before turning into the hole. The quarterback very deliberately "rides" the fullback before exchanging the ball with him.

Because the techniques of ball-handling, timing and points of attack differ between the longside and shortside fullback belly plays, these two plays will be described separately.

We prefer to run the longside fullback belly play (36 Belly) toward a slot. Since the defense is usually overshifted toward the long side, the use of the slot will force the opposition to defend a greater lateral area than it normally would. The defensive end must retain his basic outside responsibility and his position thus precludes any value he might have had to help defend in the slot area to his inside. Therefore, having made the end most aware of his outside responsibility with the threat of the outside belly option, we can attack without actually blocking him. The slot spacing has removed him from the point of attack quite effectively. Thus we have basically established a favorable four-blockers-to-three-defenders ratio at the attack point. The important factor of strength in this situation, and a good reason for its consistent performance, is the built-in possibility of a double team block. The spacing effect of the slot upon the defensive end releases the strong tackle to provide manpower for a double team block.

The "ride" method is employed effectively as a ball-handling method in teaching the longside fullback belly play. This technique strongly tends to freeze the defenders at the off-tackle hole, as they are uncertain as to who will finally be the actual ball carrier—the fullback, quarterback or perhaps the trailing halfback who is in the optional pitch-out position. No matter what the indecision should be, the inside defenders must stay at home in order to protect their basic area of responsibility.

Why the 36 Belly Play Is Effective

There are three positive factors contributing to the effectiveness of the fullback belly play: (1) the spacing which thins out the defense for better daylight running; (2) the double team block, which adds needed power and provides valuable time for the ball carrier to arrive at the line of scrimmage; and (3) the ride effect which causes indecision in the defensive reaction. The ride will also tend to freeze the perimeter or secondary defenders. They can see the ball go to the fullback but must expect the QB to take it back and continue with his option play toward the flank. The secondary men cannot commit themselves to early support of the fullback belly play.

PLAYERS' RESPONSIBILITIES
FOR THE LONGSIDE 36 BELLY

Following are the details and techniques taught for the longside fullback belly play:

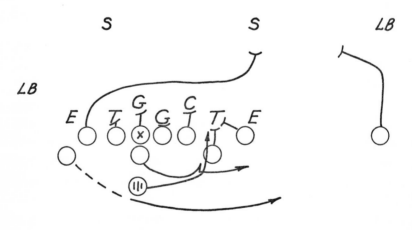

DIAGRAM 28.   36 Belly.

Quarterback

The quarterback must be a magician with the ball and must play the role of an actor up to the hilt. He is responsible for making the fullback belly play resemble its companion play, the outside belly option.

Immediately upon receiving the ball from the center, the quarterback reverse pivots on his right foot, gaining depth rapidly toward the anticipated course of the fullback. (Some play series dictate the simple open-out move for the quarterback; but it is believed that the reverse pivot throws him quicker and deeper away from the line of scrimmage—all desirable features in the belly series.)

He should reach out for the fullback with the ball in both hands. Contact with the fullback's belly and the football should be made as the FB makes his turn toward the line of scrimmage approximately 3½ yards from the line (the FB started 4 yards back). The correct angle from the line of scrimmage for the quarterback's course is 45 degrees. He must reach out for the fullback, thrust the ball into his belly, and then continue with the fullback for one full step to create the "ride" effect. The QB's step is actually a lateral shuffle which parallels the fullback's course toward the line of scrimmage.

At this point the quarterback releases the ball to the fullback, removes his hands and sprints for three strides behind him, directly at the defensive end before turning upfield. At the same time he should be studying the end's moves to determine his reaction to the belly aspect of the play. If the end is moving toward the fullback in the off-tackle hole, the quarterback should be considering the outside option play very soon.

Fullback

The fullback must take a lead step with his right foot laterally toward the sideline as he gets underway on the snap count. His second step, taken with the left foot, directs him slightly toward the line of scrimmage. On the third step he should be gaining ground toward the line of scrimmage at approximately a 30 degree course from the lateral line on which he started.

As he makes his move toward the line, his arms and hands should be in the receiving position. The inside elbow should be lifted high and the right hand held underneath at belt level to be used as a stopper to trap the ball.

Until the fullback actually gets the ball he is not moving at full speed. He should run at approximately ½ to ¾ speed, no faster, in order to make a good connection with the quarterback and to set up the "ride." The quarterback's timing and course should allow him to place the ball in the fullback's belly just as the FB plants his right foot on his third step. The "ride" commences at this point and the fullback should turn directly toward the line of scrimmage, holding up his head and eyes, looking for daylight and running room. The ride will force the fullback a trifle wider and, to offset this pressure, he must lower his inside (left) shoulder to insure deception as well as keep him on his course perpendicular to the line of scrimmage.

The fullback normally takes two steps in the ride after which the quarterback releases the ball to him. By this time, the defense has been frozen or blocked and the daylight holes have appeared in the defensive line. The fullback should run to the daylight and be prepared to cut back to his left, against the grain. We have discovered that the percentages are with the fullback who cuts back rather than runs toward the outside flank. If there is no clearly defined daylight, he should unhesitatingly blast directly behind the double team power block and drive for all available yardage.

Left Halfback

The left halfback lines up in his regular wingback position one yard outside of the left, or short side, end and one yard off the line of scrimmage. Anticipating the snap count, he starts to fly back in motion aiming at a spot one yard behind the fullback. When the ball is snapped, the left halfback should be moving laterally with only a slight angle away from the line of scrimmage. Every move and controlled action he makes is very important to the belly series play pattern.

The left halfback should time the start of his motion so that he has taken three steps before the ball is snapped. His first step is merely a directional one, an opening out movement much the same as a pulling lineman uses to get underway behind the line.

In the 36 belly play, the left halfback starts with his right foot leading, then takes two full steps before the ball is snapped. He is then one yard deeper than the fullback and one yard to his left. The halfback must run under control, which for most players limits their speed to about ¾. Having reached the maximum depth of his course (5-6 yards), the flying halfback flattens out and runs toward the sideline. Since the fullback belly play must resemble the option play to the outside, the left halfback must be in position to receive an easy pitch-out, even on the 36 belly play, which does not involve him as a potential ball carrier. (The details of his exact position at this stage of the belly series will be discussed in the section devoted to 29 Belly, the outside option.)

After the quarterback has ridden the fullback and releases the ball to him, the left halfback should turn the corner at full speed, sprinting downfield to form part of the blocking screen for the ball carrier.

Right Halfback

The right halfback is the slotback for the fullback belly play to the long side, as well as being the post man for the vital double team power block.

Normally the right halfback assumes a laterally central position in the slot. There are assignments for which he should vary his spacing in the slot, but for 36 Belly he should be in the center of a 2½-yard slot. It is imperative that the halfback, in the role of post blocker, stop any penetration charge of the defender across from him. The most serious thing that can happen to the execution of the fullback belly play is to allow penetration at the point of attack.

The right halfback must aim his head at the crotch of the defender. Upon contact he should attempt to close the gap between his strong tackle, to his outside, to avoid their being split apart by the charge of their opponent. The halfback is not instructed to try to move the defender in any specific direction, but only to drive him back off the line of scrimmage. To control the point of attack is the sole purpose of the double team power block. It is the fullback's job to find a daylight hole and make yardage.

Left End

As the ball is snapped, the left end must clear the line of scrimmage free of contact, if at all possible, in order to speed up his downfield roll. After releasing, the shortside end stays as close to the line of scrimmage as possible while still avoiding contact. Once the end acquires a lateral position in front of the point of attack, he turns downfield and throws a rolling block at the first opponent in the secondary defense. This will usually be a safety man.

Downfield blockers are taught to roll three times after making contact at knee level. With the rolling technique, even if the defender is not completely erased, there is a bonus effect of distraction and nuisance value wrought upon the defender who has a minor tornado broiling around his feet. Other than this special coaching point, downfield blocking involves the two intangibles that are ever-present in a football player: desire and hustling effort.

The left end's assignment is stressed as a vital one, never a chance to rest because the play is directed toward the other side of his line. His effort will be the key to the breakaway runs made on the fullback belly play.

Left Guard

The shortside guard must avoid letting the defensive man across from him get any quick penetration. He should shoulder-block his opponent for one full count before releasing downfield. His course to get over in front of the play should be no deeper than three yards until he reaches his fullback's point of attack. At this point, the guard turns directly upfield and throws a rolling block on the first defender to cross his path. If there is no defender readily available without a long chase, the guard should peel back to cut down a pursuing defender. This latter block is the one that linemen love best of all, and it can have a devastating effect upon pursuit.

Center

The center has a man-for-man assignment, for he must block the defender across from him, whether he be a lineman or a linebacker. His job is to prevent penetration and then retard pursuit. The center's charge is quick, but conservatively aimed high at his opponent's numbers. He strives to maintain contact to keep the defensive man off balance and delay his attempts to get over to the point of attack. If the center happens to lose contact he should use a crossbody block in a last effort to cut down the defender. Or, should a good angle be gained by quickness of charge, the center should use a body block to erase his opponent immediately.

Right Guard

The right guard must pin down his opponent in a delaying action. He does not necessarily have to eliminate or move his man, but he must keep him from getting to the attack point as quickly as the ball carrier does.

The guard should fire out directly at his opponent, aiming his head at the belt buckle. As contact is made, the feet follow up in short choppy steps and the guard slips his head to the right side, placing his head between the defensive man and the point of attack. The head and forearm act as levers to control the opponent. Position is not acquired by any false steps or by aiming the shoulder at the hip of the defender; but only after making straight-ahead contact does the guard seek position.

The head slips to the hip of the opponent and then the body is swung around to that side through use of lateral choppy steps and quick footwork. His job is to keep the defender occupied and driven away from the off-tackle hole if possible.

Inside Tackle

This lineman is very close to the point of attack for the fullback belly play and, as such, he must keep his opponent very busy and tied up, maintaining contact to permit the ball carrier to find daylight running room. He is advised to fire out in a fairly high charge for improved balance.

A clean miss of contact is extremely serious and so the inside tackle uses a more cautious, though aggressively strong, approach. Upon contact, he blocks the defensive man in the direction of least resistance, making certain to maintain contact with scrambling footwork until the whistle blows, ending the play.

Strong Tackle

Against the particular defense shown in Diagram 28, the strong tackle is the drive man in a double block while his partner, the slot halfback, is the post blocker.

From his position 2½ yards from the inside tackle (thus forming the slot), the strong tackle aims his helmet at the outside hip of the defender aligned on the slot back. He maintains a position very close to his partner throughout the block as he aids in preventing the defender from splitting the tandem block. There is no attempt to drive the opponent down the line of scrimmage, although he may be so moved. Instead, the double block should serve to control the point of attack and drive the defender straight back. This approach to the double team block has a number of advantages; namely:

1. Facilitates instruction and permits individual variances of charge by the blocking partners.

2. Coordination between the drive and post blockers is not critical.

3. The double team block serves as a deep screen to cut off pursuit.

4. Permits the ball carrier to apply his general rule of running to daylight with no pre-set notion as to where the hole will open.

Spread End

The right end releases on all plays as if a pass pattern had been called. This move forces the defender to drop back with him. About 8 to 10 yards downfield, the spread end is in-

structed to turn sharply to the inside to block a safety man in
the secondary. This maneuver amounts to a nutcracker effect
on the safety, because he is also the target of the offside linemen
who have released downfield. A good block by the spread end
is often the key to long yardage. He usually has an excellent
angle on his opponent and, therefore, can employ a shoulder
block instead of the usual rolling downfield block recommended for the open-field situation.

A Blocking Variation

If the defensive end stops the fullback belly play, the first
thought is to call the outside belly option. However, a change
in blocking assignments will also be effective. The defensive
end probably had closed fast to the inside when the strong
tackle blocked down on the defender being doubled. The
change in blocking thus indicated is to assign someone to block
the defensive end.

The strong tackle, instead of doubling with the slot man,
blocks the end, usually by turning out on him with a near
shoulder block. This adjustment removes the possibility of a
double block and with it goes the power it would generate. It

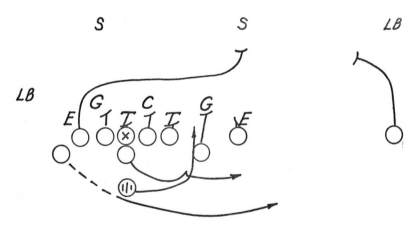

DIAGRAM 29.   36 Belly (Man-for-Man Blocking)

also places the slot man in a man-for-man situation, perhaps against a defensive tackle. However, some defenses place a linebacker across from the slotback, in which situation a fairly good halfback can handle his responsibility of keeping his opponent off balance.

This same blocking pattern can be used with the outside belly play, and the inside-out pressure on the defensive end acts as the bait to cause him to fight toward the fullback, who does *not* end up as the ball carrier.

A Formation Variation

Although the double wing slot formation has produced the most yardage for the 36 belly play, the longside fullback belly play has enjoyed some success when executed from "Peel" formation without using a man in motion.

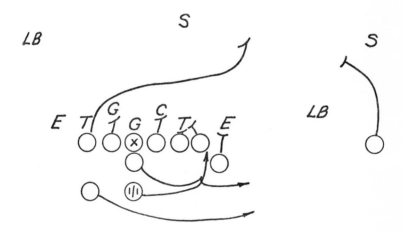

DIAGRAM 30.   Peel Right 36 Belly.

10

The Longside
Belly Option Play

THE OUTSIDE BELLY option play is the other half of the basic running attack as directed at the long side of the unbalanced line. After establishing the fullback play as a constant threat off-tackle, many long gains and scoring runs have been made by use of the outside belly option (48 Belly). During one complete season of ten games, 48 Belly averaged more than 6 yards per carry and was 80 per cent consistent. This indicates that the play, on four out of every five attempts, gained at least 3½ yards.

48 Belly Should Look Like 36 Belly to the Opponent

In order to be effective and spring the ball carrier for the surprise long gainers, the outside belly option must resemble the fullback belly play as closely as possible. The defensive team should not be able to differentiate until after the ride aspect of the series has been completed. After a few successful off-tackle runs by the fullback, it requires a well-disciplined defensive end not to be drawn eventually to the inside where the fullback is attacking.

The fullback belly play (36 Belly), when effective and frequently used, has the tendency to attract all the attention of the defenders to the point of attack. The linemen and linebackers seem to be drawn to the area much the same as high pressure air is sucked into a vacuum. If not actually drawn to the spot, the ride phase will cause indecision and a definite hesitancy in the defensive reaction. The net result is to set up the outside belly option play because the pursuit of the defense is not swift and continuous with the flow of the play and the path of the quarterback.

The normal sequence of the quarterback's strategy, when using the belly series, is to establish the fullback off-tackle play, by repetition until he feels that the defense is set up for the outsider. The fullback play is least likely to lose yardage and has a more conservative ball-handling requirement. There is little chance for a fumble as the exchange is made in a very deliberate manner under controlled movement, and the ball is handed, not tossed, from one player to another.

On the other hand, the outside belly option requires a more complex set of moves for the backs, and the ball-handling involves a pitch-out made at near full speed, decided at the last split second, and dependent upon a move by the defensive end.

Long Yardage Situations

The 48 Belly has achieved a great amount of success in long yardage situations mostly because the defense has shown a definite tendency to play soft and cautiously during the ride phase. The conservative approach on defense leaves the opponents wide open for a freeze by a good belly fake in the ride. Option plays are a very important part of the Flexible T offense and the outside belly option fits well into the general offensive pattern as the running game is established. The flanks can be attacked effectively with an option play although great halfback speed to the outside may not be available. We believe that a sound offense must be able to attack outside where the long yardage can most readily be gained. The absence of halfback speed does not preclude attacking wide; an option play is the answer. 48 Belly is an excellent option.

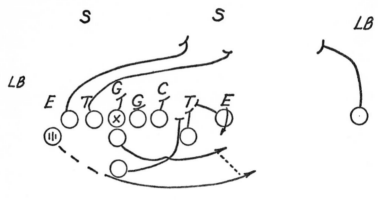

DIAGRAM 31.   48 Belly.

Blocking Similiar to 36 Belly

The diagram of 48 Belly clearly shows that the blocking assignments are similar to the pattern for 36 Belly, the other longside belly series play. It is believed that the identical blocking adds to the effectiveness and deception.

The backfield action starts the same and remains identical with the fullback belly play up to the completion of the ride. The defending linemen and linebackers are subjected to the same pressures of blocks as in the fullback play. Their reactions to what they see and feel are almost certain to be the same, and repetition would lead them to expect the off-tackle play to develop. There is additional deception, too, through the inclusion of the double team power block at the spot where the fullback concludes his fake.

Should the defensive end anticipate the outside play and drift wide, the quarterback would exercise his option, keep the ball, and cut upfield inside the defensive end who is widening with the pressure of a sweep. The double team block as applied by the slot-back and the strong tackle thus becomes a vital factor in the effectiveness of the quarterback-keeper part of the outside belly option play. The block seals off the pursuit and nails down one defender for certain, providing the quarterback with running room inside the defensive end.

It has been mentioned that man-for-man blocking is sometimes employed with the fullback belly play in an effort to keep the defensive end out of the backfield, or possibly to create a more efficient blocking pattern should the slotback be able to handle his opponent singly. This one-on-one type of blocking can also be used quite effectively with 48 Belly. The key block is that of the strong tackle who must execute a special type of block which requires an extra amount of practice for technique development. He uses the turnout pressure and reverse block.

The tackle turns out on the defensive end making contact with his near (right) shoulder. The end, feeling pressure from the inside and simultaneously seeing the fullback with the ball in the ride phase, fights inward. At this instant, the strong tackle reverses his body by quick footwork to gain an advantage in a reverse body block. While the switch from a right shoulder

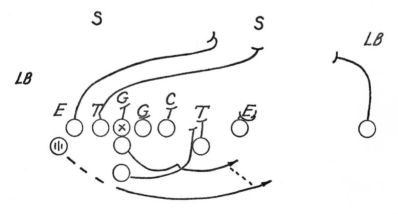

DIAGRAM 32.   48 Belly (Man-for-Man Blocking)

block to a right-side body block is being accomplished, contact is maintained, and the defensive end is hooked. The end is then rendered extremely vulnerable to the quarterback's option and the pitch-out to the trailing left halfback.

ASSIGNMENTS BY POSITION FOR THE 48 BELLY

Quarterback

The quarterback has a most important job to do and unless he can perform well, the play seldom will be a success.

The reverse pivot and course to reach the fullback remain the same as in the fullback belly play (36 Belly). The big difference between 36 and 48 Belly takes place as the quarterback extends the ball out to the fullback's belly. He does not ride the FB with a lateral shuffling of his feet as he does in the fullback belly play. His hands go along with the ball and his head and eyes follow the fullback's progress. The quarterback is cautioned not to step along with his fullback because such a maneuver would cause the QB virtually to stop all of his lateral movement. Until he could get underway again, power and speed would be lost and the quarterback's effectiveness as a ball carrier would be seriously hampered.

It is important that the quarterback *make the defensive end commit* either to play him as the present ball carrier, or to respect the trailing halfback as a potential runner. The QB is instructed to remain within 2 yards of the line of scrimmage after taking the ball back out of the fullback's belly and striding behind the FB, who is driving toward the off-tackle area. Close proximity to the line of scrimmage will make it easier for the quarterback to dash through daylight inside the defensive end, should he decide to run the keeper play.

The coaching point to be emphasized in teaching the option technique to the quarterback is for him to make a definite move

Ben Martin's
FLEXIBLE T
OFFENSE

PLATE NO. 1
"A good center snap is the start of a good offensive play."

PLATE NO. 2
"Security in ball exchange demands a firm grip on the ball by the quarterback."

PLATE No. 3
"The military huddle makes certain that every player gets the orders from the signal caller."

PLATE NO. 4
"Consistency in ball exchange requires constant rehearsal."

PLATE NO. 5
"The Oklahoma Drill teaches several fundamental skills; ball exchange, one-on-one blocking, and "daylight" running."

PLATE NO. 6

"The lead foot is the passer's direction finder and must be carefully placed for accuracy."

PLATE NO. 7

"The pass thrown to the left must not cause the passer to throw across his body." (Note the good foot placement and high start of the throwing motion.)

PLATE NO. 8

"Opening out to throw to his right the passer retains full balance throughout the throwing motion."

PLATE No. 9
"An excellent open field maneuver for the ball carrier is a cutback against the grain."

"The outside belly play, or quarterback option, requires precision timing and exact spacing. Here the quarterback has just cleared behind the fullback (35) and is in excellent position with his halfback (27) to put pressure on the defense."

after deciding to pitch out or keep the ball. Indecision on the part of the quarterback is a big problem while first learning the option technique. It is the defensive end who should be indecisive, not the quarterback. The burden of a committing move must be placed upon the opponent. A definite fake or movement by the quarterback aids the situation to the offensive team's favor.

As the quarterback becomes more proficient, he may keep the ball, gain ground across the line of scrimmage and execute an option on a secondary defender, such as a corner linebacker or halfback. However, if the quarterback decides to pitch, he must look at the target halfback before lateraling the ball. The practice of looking before pitching will save many anxious moments and remove much of the danger involved in a full speed pitch-out. The blind pitch is not recommended and the quarterback is advised to toss the ball gently, controlling it with both hands in an underhanded throwing motion. The ball should be laid out softly, easy to catch, in front of the left halfback who can field it without breaking stride.

Fullback

The fullback's course and pattern remain virtually the same as if his off-tackle belly play had been called. He moves laterally for three controlled steps before turning toward the line of scrimmage. He makes a pocket for the ball to be placed on his belt buckle and lowers his inside shoulder to hide the ball exchange.

There are several coaching points for the fullback to remember, especially since he is now the biggest actor in the backfield. He is responsible for making the defense believe that he has the ball in 48 Belly.

It is imperative that the fullback not develop any sign of laziness in carrying out his fake. Every step and move must be exactly the same as when he carries the ball on 36 Belly. The precise timing up to the completion of the ride must be preserved. The fullback must not clamp down on the ball, because the quarterback is to retain full control of it throughout the belly fake. The FB should grasp the ball as gently as if it were made of fragile china. In lowering his left shoulder, he should be careful not to curl back too much toward the center. Should he alter his course inward instead of driving straight ahead, the quarterback will find it extremely difficult to remove the ball from his grasp.

The fullback should be the most effective blocker in 48 Belly, merely by executing a good belly fake and freezing the defensive interior line. After the short side has been completed, and if he has not been tackled, the fullback should pick out an opponent straight ahead or to his inside and block him to cut down on the opponent's pursuit.

Left Halfback

Basically, the left halfback's job is the same for 48 Belly as in 36 Belly except that he is now a potential ball carrier, should the quarterback decide to pitch out. Because of this additional responsibility, the halfback must position himself much more precisely with the quarterback after going in motion to start the play.

The left halfback has the sole responsibility to maintain the correct angle and distance between himself and the quarterback to provide for the very best option situation.

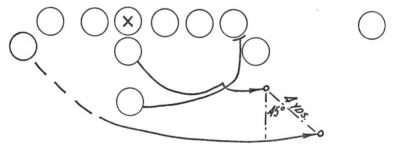

DIAGRAM 33.   Option Positioning.

If he should get too close to the quarterback, one defender (the defensive end) can usually stop both men in a zone-type coverage. Should the pitch-out man get too far away from the quarterback, the lateral pass becomes more difficult and dangerous. In both situations of incorrect halfback positioning, fumbles are invited. Best results are obtained when the left halfback is positioned 4 yards from the quarterback and in advance of him at a 45 degree angle, as shown in Diagram 33.

The early start in motion and ahead of the snap count puts the left halfback in position one yard behind and one yard to the left of the fullback. This spot serves well as the halfback's first check point. Speed control is the solution to correct position. The next critical point is reached when the quarterback completes the ride with the fullback and takes his first lateral step toward the defensive end. At this time the quarterback may have to pitch out quickly because the defender has pressured him in a penetrating move. Thus, the left halfback must be in good position to handle the pitch-out at this very moment.

Should the quarterback elect to keep the ball and turn up the field, the left halfback should also turn the corner. He must make certain to control his speed and watch the quarterback's progress closely for the possibility of a second option situation.

The delayed pitch-out in the opponent's secondary is an extremely valuable aspect of 48 Belly and results in many of the play's long gains. The left halfback must be particularly alert to the course of the quarterback, who, in a keeper play situation, flattens out immediately after eluding the end, and runs toward the sideline. The tactic indicated is an optional pitch-out using the defensive wingman as the target, a very profitable stratagem.

Right Halfback

The right halfback is the slotback for the 48 Belly play. He normally has the key blocking role of post man in a double team block with the strong tackle. His task is the same as for 36 Belly, despite the fact that the fullback will not be carrying the ball. Of course, the slotback may have to block in a man-for-man pattern as a variation of his regular assignment.

As was stated earlier, the line's blocking assignments are identical with those given them in the fullback belly play (36 Belly). Therefore, those details will not be repeated, but reference can be taken to them in this chapter under the longside belly series.

A Variation to 48 Belly

An effective variation to the outside belly option is the Power Keeper. It is especially designed for use on the goal line, or any other short yardage situation.

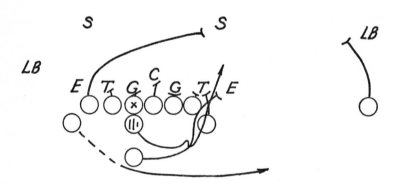

DIAGRAM 34.   Power Keeper.

The basic ingredient of the 48 Belly Power Keeper is the quarterback's course as a ball carrier, using the fullback as a personal interferer. The ride is extremely quick and the fullback stops faking immediately after the quarterback removes the ball from his belly. The fullback does not lower his inside (left) shoulder at all and does not continue to run under control. He blasts into the line at the off-tackle point of attack or leads the ball-carrying quarterback through any daylight hole he may spot. The quarterback regains complete possession of the football after a short ride, turns toward the line of scrimmage right on the tail of the fullback, his bodyguard, using him as a screen.

This power keeper play starts out with all the fine deceptive elements of the belly series and ends up with the added weapon of a valuable lead blocker for the ball carrier.

The Longside Belly Pass

In addition to the bread-and-butter running plays of a basic series, complete with all of their blocking variations, a truly effective series must have a counter-play. The belly series counter-play, 29 Reverse Belly, will be covered in the shortside belly attack, Chapter 11. A good play series must also include a pass pattern run off the play-action of the series. In the longside attack, this play is called 48 Belly Pass.

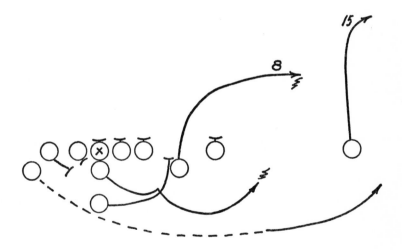

DIAGRAM 35.   48 Belly Pass.

The basic protection given to the quarterback is that of the system's play-action protection. On a play-action pass such as

48 Belly Pass, the "on" side blocks aggressively while the "off" side blocks passively in the regular type of pass protection. The details of action-type pass protection will be covered in detail in Chapter 12. In general, the "on" side fires out, then recovers, and the "off" side (in this instance, the short side) drops back to form a protective cup which prevents pursuit from behind.

The left end is shown to be a blocker in Diagram 35, which responsibility he frequently has in the unbalanced-line T pass offense. However, the shortside end might very well be released to run a pattern; but when he does, his blocking chore is usually assumed by the wingback. In 48 Belly Pass, the wingback is flying back in motion, therefore the end must block.

The essence of the 48 Belly Pass is to put a lot of pressure on the strongside flat defenders and present the quarterback with a number of potential receivers in his field of vision, as well as give him the option of running with the ball. The pressure on the strong flat is created by three receivers flooding the zone. The spread end clears through the flat and runs a flag route, breaking deep for the sideline at about 15-20 yards depth. The right halfback, who has lined up in the slot, but who also might be "peeled" as a right wingback, runs a flare-out course at a depth of 6-8 yards. The left halfback has started in motion as soon as the team is set. The quarterback uses a long snap count, allowing the left halfback to reach a position at least 5 yards wide in the right flat before the ball is snapped from center. The pass pattern thus gives the quarterback three well-dispersed receivers all in plain view.

The quarterback and fullback execute a belly fake after which the FB fills in the slot area to form part of the pass protection screen. The quarterback continues laterally on his option course ready to throw the pass immediately should he be pressured by the defensive end. Normally, because he would be throwing quickly and without being able to get set, the quarterback would toss a flat pass to his left halfback in the wide flat. Should the

QB encounter no immediate pressure, he should create some of his own by turning the corner and running right up to the line of scrimmage. This move normally will cause the defender stationed in the flat to react toward the ball-carrying quarterback.

If this movement does take place, the QB should then throw a little pass to either of his halfbacks, who both are in the flat. Should the flat zone defender (probably an end dropped off on a loosened corner linebacker) stay back on pass defense, the quarterback should tuck the ball away and sprint for running yardage. By pressuring the defense with 48 Belly Pass, the quarterback has been able to call his own shot.

To insure that deception be maintained, and that the long count man-in-motion not be a give-away of 48 Belly Pass, it is recommended that the long count motion be used also with 36 Belly occasionally. The wide halfback in the flat is also effective when employed with the power keeper play near the goal line.

11

The Shortside
Fullback Belly Play

THE SHORTSIDE fullback belly play (37 Belly) is a very quick-hitting play as compared to its counterpart play to the long side.

Instead of trying to freeze defenders and finessing them by use of the ride, the shortside fullback play is designed to get by the line of scrimmage before the defensive lineman can react to the fullback's course.

The greater number of opponents normally are aligned to the long side of the unbalanced line in an overshifted defense. 37 Belly is designed to strike quickly at a point away from the massed defenders. To quote a famous military man, the shortside fullback belly play wants to "get there firstest with the mostest."

Once again the blocking pattern is designed to take advantage of a double team block at the point of attack. The blocking ratio is 3 to 2 in favor of the offense since the pattern is set up to leave the outside defender unblocked on the line of scrimmage. Should the defensive end not be responsible for the flank and thus contribute to stopping the fullback play off-tackle, a blocking pattern would be set up to handle him. However, the usual procedure would be to exploit the undefended flank by utilizing the outside belly option play.

108

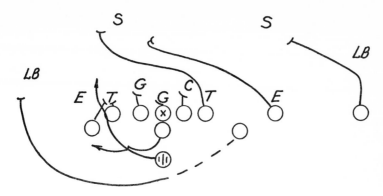

DIAGRAM 36.   37 Belly.

INDIVIDUAL TECHNIQUES FOR THE 37 BELLY

Quarterback

The quarterback starts the backfield play action by pivoting in a reverse fashion on his left foot. As in the longside belly plays, his course is 45 degrees from the line of scrimmage as he moves to intercept the fullback's course. But the fullback's course is different from the longside belly play, and the quarterback will reach him sooner than he does in the 36 Belly play to the long side. (There is very little lateral movement in the course since the fullback follows only a slightly rounded route in 37 Belly as he proceeds quickly toward the line of scrimmage.)

As the quarterback feeds the ball into the fullback's belly, he does not parallel the course of the fullback by lateral shuffling of his feet as he does in 36 Belly to the long side. There is no real ride effect because the desired timing is extremely fast and a ride would require time. The only aspect of the ride to be employed is that of the quarterback's hands, which do proceed along with the ball and the fullback.

The hands are drawn along by the ball which, at the exchange point, belongs 90% to the fullback. The 10% possession retained by the quarterback gives to the defense a slight indication of a ride effect. The quarterback also follows the fullback with his head and eyes to accentuate the fake. He ducks his inside (right) shoulder behind the fullback. It is a brief, but sharp, movement which has an additional small freezing effect upon the reaction of the defense.

The quarterback, just as the fullback, should be running at full speed on this quick-hitting play to the short side. The ride effect at ball exchange resembles a small collision as the quarterback is jerked momentarily off balance. He should not contribute to the collision impact illusion by getting his footwork involved. Rather, he should proceed on his own direct course, behind the fullback. Despite the fact that his hands are going along with the fullback, his head is following the fullback's course and his inside shoulder has been jerked down. Once the ball exchange has been completed (this usually takes only the time required for the fullback to advance one full stride), the quarterback regains his balance and sprints laterally for two or three steps before turning upfield or faking a pitch-out to his trailing halfback.

The entire picture of the moves of the quarterback in the shortside fullback belly play is one of quickness, speed, and even haste. The contrast with the longside play is quite marked and the effect of the change in timing upon the defense is very effective. Once again, the quarterback must become the actor and be well aware of the reaction of the flank defenders after he has given the ball to the fullback. A really long gainer may be set up in such a manner by the use of the comparison play to the 37 Belly; namely, the outside belly option play.

Fullback

The course for the fullback on the shortside belly play differs greatly from the one prescribed for 36 Belly to the long side. As has been stressed, quick striking power is the key to success of the 37 Belly. The fullback should line up at the regular depth of 4 yards from the ball. To start his pattern, he lead-steps with his left foot toward the point of attack.

37 Belly is not exactly a direct slant at the off-tackle spot, and the fullback must include some arc to his course. He should round it out a trifle while not hesitating in his route to the line of scrimmage. The fullback is given an exact spot at which to aim. It is the outside foot of our shortside end.

The reason for having the fullback follow a mildly rounded course is to provide him the opportunity to run to daylight. He must hit the line perpendicularly in order to be free to cut right or left, wherever the daylight should appear. A direct slant course would not give him such an opportunity, since the cut-back to the inside would be a veer of more than 90 degrees, a difficult maneuver to execute at full speed.

The basic techniques for receiving the ball are emphasized: inside elbow up, other hand in position to act as a stopper while the head and eyes are up, looking for a hole to open up along the line of scrimmage. The fullback knows that there will be no ride by the quarterback and so he grasps the ball firmly when first offered by the QB. The fullback lowers his inside (right) shoulder, which aids his course to shape up at a right angle to the line of scrimmage. The lowered shoulder also provides deception for the ball exchange, but does not slow down the fullback who is intent upon arriving at the point of attack at full speed and in a good hitting position.

Right Halfback

The right halfback lines up in his regular slotback position, or just slightly cheated in toward his inside tackle. This will place him relatively the same distance from the center as a wingback would be on the short side. The positioning is important because of the timing of the halfback as he flies back in motion.

Anticipating the snap count, he starts in motion to his left, aiming at a spot one yard behind the fullback. When the ball is snapped, the right halfback should be moving laterally with only a slight angle away from the line of scrimmage. He should time his start so that he has taken three steps before the ball is put into play.

The first step is merely an opening-out movement with the left foot serving to throw him back and to his left. It sets the exact direction of his course behind the fullback. The second and third steps will place him one yard deeper than the fullback and one yard to his right when the ball is snapped. Running at ¾ speed to be able to control his spacing and preserve the timing of the play, the halfback flattens out toward the sideline after reaching the maximum depth in his course of 5-6 yards from the line of scrimmage. He is then in good position to receive a pitch-out, which will not be forthcoming in the 37 Belly play, but will be a distinct possibility when the companion play, 29 Belly, is run.

The two plays must look exactly alike until the ball exchange is completed. After the fullback has the ball and is hitting the line, the right halfback turns the corner at full speed in an effort to get into the blocking pattern downfield.

Left Halfback

The left halfback is the drive man in the double team block. He executes his responsibility from the normal wingback position, one yard off the line of scrimmage and one yard outside his left end. It is imperative that he charge in a direct line at the defender's nearest hip. (The defender is normally lined up opposite the shortside end.)

In taking a straight-line course to his inside, the halfback should anticipate the forward charge of his opponent. The correct course will place the halfback's helmet on the defender's hip, after which the helmet will slide to the outside, behind the defender, for the completion of the contact for a good near-shoulder block.

In order to accomplish his role, the left halfback leads with his right foot in a short directional step and follows with choppy steps on course. By the third step he should make contact with his helmet and right shoulder up close to his neck, not out on the end. The impact is intensified by the coordination, at the very instant of contact, of an armlift. The contact with the forearm does much to knock the defender off balance. Aiming at the hip provides an excellent contact point for controlling an opponent with power. Should the halfback take a rounded course before making contact, valuable time will be lost, power in the charge dissipated, and the defender might possibly split apart the double team and penetrate across the line of scrimmage.

Once again, the major objective of the block is to move the defender back off the line of scrimmage and therefore control the point of attack of the 37 Belly play. It is often found that a good double team block is an effective means of cutting off pursuit, as a screen is formed at the point where the ball carrier crosses the line of scrimmage.

Left End

The shortside end is the post man for the double team block. It is imperative that he stop all penetration of the defender, who will usually direct his charge through the left end. The defender's charge must be neutralized at the line of scrimmage. Then when his partner makes contact, their combined effort and power is used to drive back the opponent. The shortside end must drive his helmet low and hard directly at the crotch of his opponent. After contact, the end must not only turn on the power to move the defender but must also maneuver to avoid being split away from his partner in the block. Such a split would permit penetration across the line and prevent control of the line of scrimmage at the vital point of attack.

As always, it is the fullback's job to run to daylight and find the hole wherever it should open. The left end is directed normally to space himself about 2-3 feet from his shortside guard. This alignment affords comfortable spacing and spreads the defense just enough to provide running room for the ball carrier. Any tighter spacing would make it difficult to identify true daylight for the fullback. Any greater spacing would invite penetration through a gap by the defensive man. Wide spacing by the left end would also move the point of attack too wide for a quick thrust by the fullback in the 37 Belly play.

Left Guard

The shortside guard's main objective is to pin down his opponent immediately to nullify quick pursuit and prevent penetration. His offensive charge is aimed directly at the middle of his opponent, making crisp contact before trying for position on the outside hip.

The guard is trying to neutralize the defender with a "butt" block before driving him in the direction of least resistance. He makes certain to maintain close contact for as long as possible to give the fullback ample time to run to daylight through the line of scrimmage. This is especially true should the hole open up inside the double team block, for then the guard's opponent would be the most dangerous defender to upset the ball carrier. Should contact by the left guard be lost, the cross body block should be used in a last effort to cut down the opponent or bother him to the extent that he cannot get set to make a strong tackle.

Center

The center's assignment is to block the man across from him, whether he be a lineman or a linebacker. He must prevent penetration and retard pursuit. If his opponent is a lineman, the center normally would attempt to hook him with a quick body block that would place his body between the opponent and the point of attack. The center's head is the controlling factor in the hook-style of block as he shoots his helmet for the hip of his opponent. It is recommended that all centers work extra time in building up their neck muscles to insure adequate strength to handle an opponent with the head. Bridging exercises are excellent neck muscle builders, or at times a weight-lifting program can be outlined by the coach or trainer, especially designed for aspirant centers.

In blocking a linebacker, the center charges directly at the numbers on the jersey, executing a high shoulder block. Such a technique will keep the linebacker off balance and, being a conservative charge, will insure good contact. A complete miss would be a serious mistake; thus a belt-high or lower shoulder block is not recommended.

Should the linebacker be extremely quick in his lateral reaction, or play back off the line further than normal, the center would probably have to direct his charge toward the point of attack in an effort to head off the linebacker. In this instance, the cross body technique should be used with the head still placed between the opponent and the ball carrier. The center does not have to move his opponent out of the way, but merely pin him down or busily keep him off balance in a fashion that will reduce his effectiveness as a tackler.

Right Guard

The right guard must strive to eliminate the opponent across from him as a tackler. More often than not, that player is a linebacker and is the most likely man to get into position to stop the shortside belly play.

The reverse pivot move made by the quarterback should delay the defender briefly, allowing the guard to explode off the line charging directly at the opponent. He uses a high shoulder block aimed at the jersey numbers in an effort to drive the linebacker backwards and off balance. If the linebacker has already reacted laterally, the guard should not hesitate to make contact, even should it be on the defender's back because the rules spell out the legality of clipping in the normal zone for linebackers. The important object for the guard is to make contact and keep the opponent off balance, thus reducing his effectiveness as a tackler even should he get a hand on the ball carrier. The guard must stay with his man with a great amount of scrambling and concentrated effort.

Inside Tackle

The inside tackle is far enough removed from this quick-hitting shortside play so that he is not required to make a block at the line of scrimmage. He releases for a downfield block and should be the first man to form the interference screen for the fullback.

The inside tackle's release course is inside, or to his own left, of any opponent whose position across from him might at first seem to force him to the outside. To conserve vital time the tackle must explode in a direct line toward the point of attack of the 37 Belly play to his left. After executing his release, in a very low, hard charge, the tackle sprints across the field, going no deeper than 3 yards until he is in front of the hole. Having reached this position, he then turns upfield and blocks the first available defender. He must not pass up any defender in his path in order to block another target further along the way. The ones who are passed up usually make the tackle.

The recommended block is the roll-up style of downfield block. This technique involves the basic cross body block aimed at the knees or thighs and augmented by three complete body rolls through the feet of the opponent.

Strong Tackle

The strong tackle (outside man) also releases for a downfield block. He releases from the line of scrimmage in exactly the same manner as the inside tackle does and sprints across the field following a shallow course to reach the point of attack. At this point the strong tackle turns upfield to enter the interference pattern for the fullback. He probably will have the opportunity to use the rolling downfield block as described above, unless he has a good angle for a shoulder block. Such an angle would only be presented when the ball carrier decides to cut back to his right and run against the flow of the defensive reaction. Should the strong tackle find no targets within reach, he should peel back to cut down the pursuers.

Spread End

The spread end is deployed wide as a potential pass-receiver and he should release on all plays as if a forward pass were to be thrown. The object is to force the secondary back and make them aware that a pass is imminent. After 4 or 5 strides on a direct course downfield, the end is instructed to veer to the inside. This change of course places the end in excellent position to form a screen block for the fullback in the shortside belly play should the ball carrier decide to cut back to his right. The cutback route is the usual one and so a good block by the spread end is often the key to real long yardage.

The end employs a shoulder block because he usually has a blocking angle advantage created by the change in direction of the fullback. The cutback sets up the secondary defenders perfectly for the spread end.

12

The Shortside
Belly Option Play

JUST AS THE fullback belly play to the short side was described as a very quick-hitting weapon, so is the outside belly option to that zone of attack. The defensive men near the point of attack have very little time as regards making a decision. The constant threat of the quick off-tackle thrusts by the fullback and the double team block puts a great amount of pressure very quickly upon the defense.

Defensive End: The Critical Man

The defensive end is the key to the success of the play and he normally will close down the line to seal off the zone immediately outside the double team block. Most defensive ends have been schooled to read an offensive block in this fashion because it normally indicates an off-tackle play directed at them. Such a move would be effective against 37 Belly and would force the offense to resort to a different kind of blocking, usually man-for-man; but the first reaction of the quarterback of the Flexible T offense would be to run the outsider, 29 Belly.

29 Belly strikes extremely fast because there is no delay at all, no slow-down in the ride, and the quarterback actually sprints

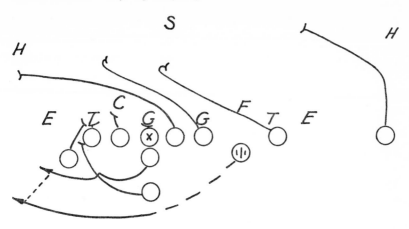

DIAGRAM 37. 29 Belly.

off the mark. He arrives immediately at the option point because 29 Belly is a shortside play with limited lateral distance to be covered before the ball carrier finds himself outside the flank. As in the longside belly series, it is well to establish the fullback play before springing the option to the outside. However, the opposite approach has been used successfully against certain defensive alignments or a particular defensive end.

For example, against an end who prefers to close quickly to his inside, the 29 Belly play would be established first. Then when the end had loosened up a bit, aware of the outside danger, 37 Belly would be sprung inside of him. The quickness of both basic plays in the shortside belly series make them extremely effective as partners in the attack.

Calling the 29 Belly at Goal Line

29 Belly has proved to be an excellent goal-line play, probably in part due to the speed of the pattern development, and partly a result of the option aspect of the play. A defensive team is less apt to make any quick defensive adjustments near the goal line, thus adding to the potential success of a belly play.

The defensive adjustments are infrequent because a team normally lines up in a special goal-line defense, which is relatively inflexible. Then, too, there is very little depth for the pass defenders to cover, and rotation with motion is a difficult maneuver to execute. Most secondary defenders would be almost forced into a man-for-man coverage by the deployment of the offense in an unbalanced line, double wing slot formation with a widely spread end.

COACHING THE BACKFIELD FOR THE 29 BELLY

The details of 29 Belly are similar to those outlined in 37 Belly and space will not be allotted to a repetition of the team's assignments. The blocking assignments for the linemen are identical, but there are a few coaching points that merit mention as regards the backfield.

Quarterback

The quarterback starts the play just as he did 37 Belly with a full speed reverse pivot at 45 degrees from the line of scrimmage. He thrusts the ball into the fullback's belly; but does not slow down in any real ride phase as he did in the longside belly option. The ball is snatched out as quickly as it was thrust in. Since the quarterback is continuing at full speed on his course behind the fullback, there is a jerky motion at this point. The quarterback's hands are behind him and to the right side, which has forced a twisting to the right of his upper body, including his head. These combined movements throw him off balance momentarily and in order to regain balance he is instructed to chop his steps, but not slow down. He must pop out of the hasty ride phase and pressure the defensive end.

The quarterback has very little time to regain his balance, sight in on the defensive end, and make a decision on the options at his disposal. He must practice many times the quick and decisive move after clearing the path of the fullback. If the end drifts or remains stationary, the quarterback normally fakes the pitch and keeps, turning up the field. Should he be pressured into pitching out quickly, he must pay particular attention to the accuracy of the lateral toss.

Remember that he may still be off-balance, have to make an extremely rapid decision, and toss an accurate lateral pass. He cannot be concerned about the impending collision, but must concentrate on pitching the ball to his speeding halfback. Once the pitch has been made, the QB is drilled on turning his back toward the defending tackler, or at least getting his hip around to absorb the blow.

Fullback

The only coaching point for the fullback in 29 Belly that differs from everything else he is directed to do in 37 Belly, involves the actual ride phase. He must be cautioned to form a larger pocket for the ball in order to make certain that the quarterback gets it into his belly. The QB is thrusting the ball out toward that pocket at full speed and without a larger pocket there is great danger of a fumble, especially from jamming the ball upon an elbow or fist. The fullback can guarantee his responsibility merely by lifting his inside elbow uncomfortably high and loosening his other hand to a lower position.

Such a loose pocket for the ball exchange position will not hinder the fullback during the short ride he gets from the quarter-back, because it is not desirable to have the fullback grasp the ball at all during 29 Belly. He should not attempt to get his hands on the ball. The quarterback will put it far enough into his belly to make an adequate fake. Any hand pressure that the fullback might exert upon the ball would increase what is already a difficult trick for the quarterback—getting the ball in and out of the ride phase while travelling at full speed!

So, the fullback must not grab at the ball at all. But the rest of his pattern remains the same as in 37 Belly.

37 BELLY PASS

In keeping with the principle of a well-balanced attack in any one series—and it is believed that the shortside belly plays are a series in themselves—a play-action pass is a prerequisite. Since a flood pattern which places three receivers in one general zone is used in conjunction with the play-action pass (48 Belly Pass) to the long side, a different type of pattern is delegated to the shortside attack. (This change in pattern does not limit the Flexible T because it must always be kept in mind that the short-side attack can be directed to the right as well as the left, merely by flopping the unbalanced line over to the other side.) The pattern selected includes only two receivers, for maximum protection to the short side, and has one deep and the other short in a spot area.

Thus, the elements of a good pattern are inherent: good pass

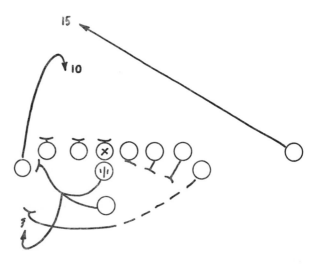

DIAGRAM 38.   37 Belly Pass.

protection, play-action for deception, a short receiver who can be hit with a timing, spot pass, a deep receiver who may break away for a score, and a pattern which tends to spring loose one of the receivers.

The protection for the passer is gained from two sources: the deception created by the action in the backfield, and the modified pass protection blocking of the line. The backs run the basic action of 37 Belly while the linemen charge aggressively for one step and then control their charge to protect for the passer.

Quarterback

The quarterback reverse pivots toward the fullback just as in 37 Belly, then after the short ride phase, he drops back to a point about 7 yards deep, laterally approximately behind the spot where his left halfback had lined up as the wingback. From there, he sets and prepares to throw to either of his two potential receivers who are both in his direct field of vision downfield.

Fullback

The fullback runs his course for 37 Belly, but immediately after the ride by the quarterback he looks for someone to block as he is an integral part of the pass protection. Basically, the fullback must protect the zone vacated by the left halfback who is one of the potential receivers. Primarily, the fullback fills to the outside of the shortside end, making certain to turn all rushers to the outside.

Right Halfback

The right halfback goes in motion to his left, just as in 37 Belly, from his slotback position. Running more under control than usual, the right halfback pulls up to a pass protection position after running by the ride spot of the fullback and quarterback. The halfback sets up at a spot wider than where his widest teammate (LHB) had lined up, and approximately 5 yards deep as a personal protector for the quarterback, who is the passer.

The right halfback is first conscious of any pressure from the outside. If none is apparent, he then turns his attention to the middle of the line and back to the long side in case there has been any leakage in the pass protection screen. He retains a good, strong, upright stance, continually moving his head back and forth to spot trouble in the shape of a rushing opponent.

Left Halfback

From his wingback position, the left halfback charges into the opponent across from him just as in 37 Belly. But he makes certain to make only momentary contact, not to get involved or delayed for more than one count because he has a pass route to run downfield.

The play-action in the backfield plus the simulated block by the wingback creates an excellent impression of a running play, especially to the linebackers. The left halfback's route in the pass pattern is designed to take full advantage of the linebacker's normal reaction to the fullback's course in 37 Belly. They tend to react to the point of attack and stay very close to the line of scrimmage, at least until the quarterback shows pass.

By that time, the left halfback has sprinted straight downfield to a depth of 10 yards. Reaching his maximum penetration into the secondary, the left halfback executes a buttonhook, or stop, maneuver. He whirls abruptly to the right after planting his left foot to be used as a pivotal point. This move faces him directly back at the passer and he must be ready to catch a spot pass immediately, as timing is vital to the 37 Belly Pass. The left halfback has hooked behind the linebackers and in front of the safety man. He is the number one target for the quarterback.

Spread End

The right end is the other potential pass receiver in the pattern and he has the role of deep man. The spread end lines up at his medium spacing (approximately 8 yards from the strong tackle) because his pattern takes him toward the opposite flank. His wide spacing would make it most difficult to cross over in time to be an effective part of the pass pattern of 37 Belly Pass.

The spread end executes a speed break, sprints at full speed, at a point 5 yards deeper than the single safety man of a 3-deep defense, or 5 yards behind the far safety of a 2-deep defense. This route will place him well beyond his left halfback who has buttonhooked at 10 yards of depth. Should the spread end burst clear as a result of his speed pattern, or because the safety man lured up to defend against the hook pattern of the left halfback, the quarterback is instructed to fake the hook pass, pump, and lift the ball up high for the spread end to run under it on a long pass.

With the basic plays to the short side, 37 Belly, 29 Belly, and 37 Belly Pass, all that is needed is a counter-play and the quarterback has a complete shortside offensive series with which to attack the enemy.

13

The Counter-Play
of the Belly Series

Every play series that proves to be productive must include some type of a counter-play. The counter-play should be designed to take full advantage of all the quick adjustments or hasty reactions the defense has made to halt the main plays in the series.

In the belly series, as used in the Flexible T, the defense is liable to make some quick perimeter adjustments as a result of the very directional flow of the basic play patterns. The flow is established by the direction of the halfback in motion and the course of the fullback once the ball is snapped. A typical quick adjustment encountered is the rapid rotation of the defensive backs toward the motion of the halfback. In this perimeter adjustment, the corner linebackers drop back when the halfback's motion is away from them and move forward to the line of scrimmage with his motion toward them. The two safety men adjust laterally with the flow of motion.

Such a drastic adjustment places the defense in a fully rotated posture; but the secondary enacts the moves because of the certainty that the ensuing play is to be aimed in the direction of the man-in-motion. A simple counter-move by the offense would be *not* to send a man-in-motion and still run the belly series

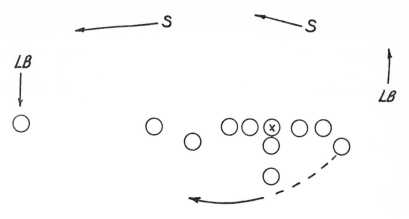

DIAGRAM 39.   Perimeter Adjustment.

plays. This can best be effected from the peel (single wingback T) formation, or by cheating the wingback back and in toward the direction of his normal motion course but not permitting him to start before the ball is snapped.

Another common reaction by the defense to the belly series is the fast keying of linebackers to the course of the fullback. It would appear that a fullback key would take the linebackers immediately to the side of the line at which the series point of attack is located. This key is fairly effective in stopping the fullback belly play but it produces the tendency on the part of the linebackers to concentrate too much attention upon the fullback at the expense of the longer gaining outside belly option play.

29 REVERSE BELLY

With these two main defensive adjustments in mind (rotation with motion and linebackers keying the fullback), a counterplay for the belly series was designed. It is 29 Reverse Belly and will be detailed as a shortside counter-play although it is run equally effectively to the long side as needed in any particular game.

29 Reverse Belly has built into it the measure necessary to neutralize the two main adjustments to the basic series as outlined above. The quick rotation, which is keyed on the direction of the left halfbacker's motion is nullified because the motion starts out in the direction *away* from the final point of attack. This play derives its name from the left halfback's course as he reverses his direction soon after starting in motion.

The linebackers' keying on the fullback is nullified because the ball also ends up in the opposite direction from the fullback's course. In the shortside 29 Reverse Belly play, the fullback's course takes him to the right, aimed at the off-tackle hole, while the ball carrier's point of attack is actually around his own left end.

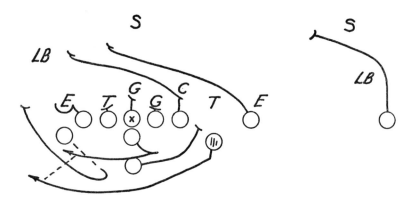

DIAGRAM 40.   29 Reverse Belly.

There are a number of influences at work upon the defense as the basic belly series is attacking them. Since 29 Reverse Belly is being aimed at the short side, it is well to spell out the reactions normally found when this counter-play is first sprung upon the opponent.

29 Reverse Belly Aims at Defensive Right End

The defensive right end is at the point of attack and, other than the perimeter defender (corner linebacker) who has already tended to rotate backward, he is the most important target of the play. As soon as the defensive end sees the wingback in front of him start in motion away from him, he has a tendency to relax because the basic belly series plays have not attacked his position once that left halfback has flown away.

Just as he makes up his mind that he is out of the immediate action area, he feels pressure in the form of a shoulder block from the inside. The offensive left end has turned out on him and will later switch around to try to hook him. (Details of this reverse influence and switch block will be given with the left end's assignment.) The defensive right end will also be subjected to a lead blocker and an option keep or pitch situation as 29 Reverse Belly develops. He has problems!

The defensive right tackle's reaction is kindled by the halfback's start in motion as well as the course that the fullback follows, both of which are in his line of vision—and the action is all away from him. The tackle's tendency is to react to his inside or at best to hold still and not charge out. Should he actually charge to the outside, he would be set up for the quick trap play, which will be described later in detail, but which also includes the fly-back motion by the left halfback.

Of course, the guards (or middle guard in an odd defense) must react to the combined false direction of the quarterback and fullback and thus will be charging away from the final point of attack. Used strictly as a counter-play and not in the role of a basic play in the series, 29 Reverse Belly has proved to be quite successful. In one season alone, the play averaged 9 yards per attempt and was more than 80 percent consistent. The high average yardage gained is a result of careful and timely use of the play as the counter to the entire belly series. Had the play been run more often, the average gain would have been less, but it would probably continue to be an extremely efficient weapon.

29 Reverse Belly includes an additional factor of strength in a counter-play, since it is another option play as it develops. The quarterback has the freedom to keep the ball himself or pitch it out to his trailing halfback, just as he could do in the regular outside belly option. The play is ideally suited for short yardage strategy when the defense would be most likely to be watching the fullback very closely. The unusual backfield action gives the illusion of confusion which is transmitted to the defenders, making them more vulnerable.

DETAILED PLAYER ASSIGNMENTS

Quarterback

The quarterback starts his pattern just as he does in 48 Belly with a reverse pivot off his right foot, throwing himself abruptly back toward the fullback on a 45 degree course. He takes one full step with his left foot, and then takes a skip move with his right before planting his left foot firmly. This footwork scheme moves him close enough to the fullback to establish the belly fake, and also puts the QB in excellent balance for the reversal of his direction.

It is not necessary that the ball be put into the belly of the fullback. The mere thrusting motion by the quarterback with the ball is sufficient for the fake as the QB does not want to be delayed any longer than it takes him to step out, skip and plant his left foot while thrusting the ball toward the fullback. At this point the quarterback reverses his direction completely and sprints to the left at a lateral depth of 3 yards behind the line of scrimmage. He is looking for the reaction of the defensive end in order to help him make his option decision of whether to keep or pitch out.

Fullback

The fullback runs a course similar to the one he follows in 48 Belly. That is, he runs under control mostly laterally for three steps before turning toward the line of scrimmage and forming a pocket for the ball. He need not expect the quarterback to put the ball into his belly, nor does he reach out for it. After the quarterback has left him, the fullback's fake is complete and he blasts into the line blocking any opponent in the area who may have penetrated in pursuit of the ball.

Left Halfback

The left halfback is normally aligned as a wingback to the short side on 29 Reverse Belly. From this spot he starts in motion to his right, making certain to be under control as regards speed and balance because he must reverse his direction after 4 short steps. He starts out with his right foot in a directional lead step which aims him a trifle behind the fullback. He takes 2 more short choppy strides before planting his left foot and reversing his course. The ball has been snapped on his third step; this timing seems to place the left halfback in ideal position to be the lead blocker for the 29 Reverse Belly play.

Upon reversing his direction, the left halfback assumes a new course which will take him about one yard outside of the defensive end. However, the halfback must be ready immediately upon reversal to block the end, who sometimes will penetrate hard after the man-in-motion, despite efforts by the shortside offensive end to block him. Quick penetration is undesirable because it removes the optional keeper play by the quarterback who must automatically pitch when pressured. Should there be no penetration by the defensive end, the left halfback will continue on course around left end, turn upfield and block the first opponent he comes across in the secondary. He is then the lead blocker and a real added strength feature to a belly option play.

Right Halfback

The right halfback is aligned as the slotback in this particular formation. The only adjustment to his normal positioning is a recommended depth improvement to approximately a yard and a half off the ball instead of the usual one yard. This added depth is required to assure that the right halfback will not collide with the fullback who is coming his way, and to place him in good option position with the quarterback later in his course. It will be recalled that the quarterback's final lateral course to the left placed him a bit deeper (3 yards) than the normal depth for the regular option play.

The right halfback will be a potential ball carrier in the 29 Reverse Belly and, as such, normally would have to start early to obtain good position for the option. But the timing works out well without an early start because the quarterback is taking 3 quick, time-consuming steps in the fake to the fullback. Those 3 steps, plus the deeper course of the halfback, provide the factors for an excellent option position as the pattern approaches the area where a decision is to be made by the quarterback.

The right halfback starts on the snap of the ball and makes certain to make his first directional step a deep one, after which he runs toward a spot 2 yards behind the fullback's original position before flattening out to parallel the lateral course of his quarterback. Just as in all option plays, the halfback is ready to receive a pitch-out, or if one is not forthcoming, he turns the corner to form part of the downfield blocking pattern, or to set up another option.

Left End

The shortside end is the only lineman whose assignment differs from the normal shortside belly play. Since he has no wingback to help him on 29 Reverse Belly, he must block in a one-on-one style. Because of the counter nature of the play and the delay involved before the ball carrier arrives at the point of attack, the left end must employ a rather special blocking technique.

It was mentioned as part of the detailed reaction on the part of the defense that the defensive right end had to contend with many problems in this play, including a "reverse influence and switch" block put on him by the offensive shortside end.

In executing the reverse influence and switch block, the left end turns out on his opponent, making contact with a near (left) shoulder block. This contact should be made higher than usual, preferably above the waist. A high contact point is more conservative, keeps balance best, and serves to screen the defender's vision as he tries to find the ball. As the left end feels pressure from the defender, who is fighting back against the influence, he immediately switches to a left side body block. In carrying on the second phase of this rather complex but extremely effective block, the left end drops to all fours, maintaining contact throughout. He scrambles in a crab move, whipping his body and legs around to an outside advantage position. The switch to a reverse body block must be made quickly and takes a great deal of practice to perfect.

The timing on the block is important but usually not difficult to acquire. At about the time the defender is exerting pressure from the outside-in, the left end starts his switch and the man-in-motion reverses his direction as does the quarterback.

The remainder of the linemen have the same blocking assignments as they had on 29 Belly. Their chores are made a bit easier because of the false reaction of the opponents across from them as they see the beginning of 29 Reverse Belly. One refinement should be mentioned, however, and that involves the offside linemen who are releasing to block downfield. They should make contact for one count before releasing to prevent immediate penetration while the false belly fake is being carried through by the quarterback and fullback.

14

Installing the Trap Series

AN OFFENSIVE SYSTEM is not complete unless some provision is made for trap blocking to be a part of it. Straight-ahead blocking, whether it involves one man against another or two men doubling up for power against a single opponent, has its limitations. This statement is particularly significant when the defenders mount a serious weight advantage.

When the defenders are physically stronger and are permitted to dig in or charge in a manner to thwart only a straight-ahead style of blocking, their physical superiority can be an insurmountable obstacle in the path of victory. Trap blocking has the effect of somewhat neutralizing any disparity in physical strength. It has a tendency to make the defenders play honest as they cannot assume that all they need do is outcharge the man across from them to control their zone of the line of scrimmage.

When a defensive lineman must be concerned about controlling his charge because of the threat of a trap block, his power is diminished and his recklessness can no longer be effectively used in a defensive charge. Thus, through restraint in his general approach, the defender becomes easier to block under all conditions.

Of course, there are players who can charge at full speed and still have reaction skills to defend against being trapped, but they are a strict minority. A smaller player can quite adequately

134

trap-block a defender because he is charging into him from the side, an angle from which the defensive man can exert little stability as compared to the resistance he can bring to bear against a frontal attack. The trap blocker is usually more effective, too, because of the surprise element. The defender normally expects pressure from an opponent nearly face to face with him. The lateral impact comes unexpectedly, especially if the target had been set up by an influence block or a particularly good backfield action fake to draw him out of position or off balance.

FOUR TYPES OF TRAP BLOCKING

There are many types of trap blocking and the Flexible T, in its effort to provide as many weapons as possible, includes the four major types. It is believed that the quarterback thus has the weapons available to make an honest man of any defender along the line. The trap blocks are all incorporated into separate play patterns and include: (1) quick trap, (2) scissors, (3) long trap, and (4) near trap. Some offensive systems include the tackle trap as an integral part of the attack, and quite efficiently. But the Flexible T asks only the guards to execute the trap blocks in order to preserve the relative simplicity of the blocking rules. Trap plays always become an exception to a lineman's general rules for blocking assignments and the guards alone are required to master the exceptions created by trap blocking.

Quick Trap

The quick trap technique is so named because the victim is the first lineman past the center to either side. The trapping guard can thus pull out of the line and be ready to block his opponent after having taken only 2 or 3 steps. The ball carrier

hits the hole immediately, without hesitation, as will be clarified
in the detailed explanation of the quick trap plays.

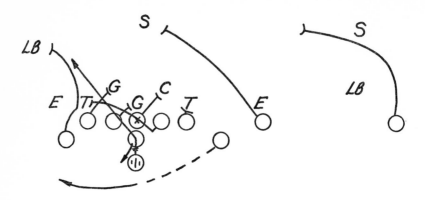

DIAGRAM 41.   Quick Trap.

Scissors

The next trap technique is actually a derivative of quick-
trapping and is dependent upon the defensive alignment. It is
the scissors technique and is to be used against an even style of
defense when a quick trap play has been called by the quarterback.

The scissors block is actually the quickest of all trap techniques because the victim of it is nearest to the guard who will
trap him. A typical situation would have a defender head-up
on the offensive guards with the center uncovered. In the definition of the quick trap, the first man past the center is the target;
thus the center would merely block away from the target defender and the pulling guard would scissor behind the center to
blast his opponent. In this situation, one or two steps would
place the guard in contact with the defender in an extremely
fast move.

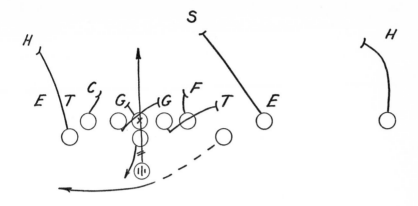

DIAGRAM 42.   Scissors.

Long Trap

The long trap is so named because the course for the pulling guard is the longest of any before contact is made with the defender being trapped. The aiming point is usually designated as the second lineman past the center, which indicates that the guard has to run 4 or 5 steps before making contact. Because the key block is made after some delay, the backfield action is not of the quick variety.

This principle is consistent with the Flexible T philosophy of varying the timing at the point of contact. The plays incorporating the long trap block are the counter trap—which has cross-action in the backfield to freeze the defense—and the back trap, which is a flow-type play somewhat like the belly series. The back-trap pattern starts out as a very directional action to the right or left, but then suddenly the ball is handed back to a trailing man who darts behind the pulling guard's long trap block.

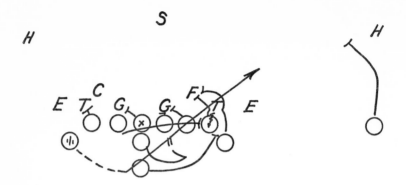

DIAGRAM 43.   Long Trap.

Near Trap

The fourth style of trap blocking, the near trap, differs from the three main styles in that the trap is executed by the guard nearest the point of attack, not the guard from the opposite side of center.

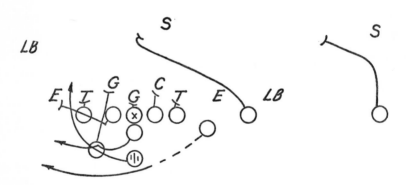

DIAGRAM 44.   Near Trap.

The near trap technique allows very quick timing and can be used quite effectively with a backfield pattern which has the fullback slanting off-tackle. In this offensive system, the near trap block is frequently used with 37 Belly.

15

Individual Assignments for the Quick Traps

THE FULLBACK QUICK trap is the fastest striking weapon in the entire system of offense and has proved to be a most effective ground-gainer. It has averaged 6.2 yards per attempt and has had a fine consistency average of 75 percent.

The 31 Trap, as it is called, provides the "fast ball" of the repertoire and, with its sprinter speed, often gets by the defenders before they can react to the pattern. It complements the average speed of the longside belly series and is a wonderful change of pace to the dropback pass attack. This is so because the linebackers tend to loosen when expecting a pass, thus making them vulnerable to a block, and the linemen charge across the line to rush the passer, making them an easy mark for the trapping guard.

All of the traps are exceptions to the daylight theory of running with the ball. The ball carriers are instructed to run specifically on the tail of the trapping guard. The traps are designed to be precision-timing plays, and complete discipline of action is required of the pulling guard and the ball carrier. Each must be confident that the other is going to execute exactly the same way each time the play is called. This teamwork and confidence to run at full speed in the pattern is built up through constant drilling in practice. The trap drill will be detailed later in this chapter.

The use of the man-in-motion is very important to the quick trap plays because the motion usually has an effect upon the linebackers, who are the most difficult opponents to block in any trap play. The Flexible T employs the man-in-motion primarily away from the direction of the trap, making the 31 Trap play somewhat of a counter pattern. This is especially true when run against an "odd" defense where the fullback's route takes him back against the grain.

If the linebackers are not the chief problem in setting up adequate blocks for the quick trap, the man-in-motion will be used to influence the defender who is to be trapped. This decision would have the halfback start to fly-back toward the trap direction with the hope that the target lineman would tend to react in the flow direction, thus becoming an easy mark for the lateral block of the pulling guard.

In some instances, the trap play has been run without any motion at all in an effort to take away all keys. When run in this manner, the quickness of the play is emphasized as it has the same effect as a pitcher throwing the ball without a windup motion.

Diagram 45 readily shows that 31 Trap's blocking pattern introduces a maximum number of angle blocks at the point of attack. These angles produce an alley through which the fullback must run. They also make effective blocks easier to obtain because physical strength is not the prime factor as it is in head-on blocking. The quick impact from the side, the precision course of the ball carrier, and the quick timing of the play make it effective.

Many times, because of the disciplined nature of the play, the fullback, running at full speed down the alley made by his teammates, gains much yardage simply by breaking through

arm tackles as the defenders are off-balance and have to resort
to reaching over blockers to try to stop the rampaging FB.

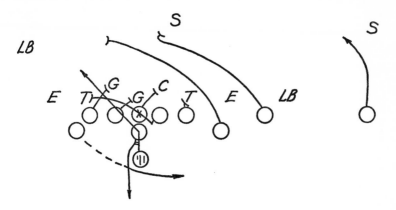

DIAGRAM 45.   31 Trap.

PLAYER ASSIGNMENTS FOR 31 TRAP

Quarterback

The basic impact of the play is in its extremely quick timing,
not deception in ball-handling, nor an intricate backfield action.
Thus, the chief responsibility of the quarterback becomes one
of sure ball-handling.

The exchange is made at full speed and the responsibility lies
completely with the quarterback to make certain that the fullback gets the ball in a good exchange. The quarterback pivots
on the foot nearest the point of attack. In this instant the play
(31 Trap) is aimed at the left side of center and the quarterback
pivots on his left foot. This move amounts to a reverse pivot
as he turns his back to the defender who will be trapped. He
should stagger his feet at least to the heel-and-toe position to
insure clearing back away from the line of scrimmage on the
snap. This detail will clear a path for the trapping guard who

must feel free to blast laterally at full speed, not being at all concerned with any teammates being in the way.

Other than the ball exchange, the quarterback is most interested in getting out of the path of the fullback, whose aiming point is right at the ball. To assure clearance, the quarterback pivots around almost to the 45 degree angle he used in the belly series. This exaggerated reverse pivot will open him out and remove him quickly from the path of the fullback. The QB does not carry the ball back toward the fullback. He merely opens out and lays the ball out in his left hand for the fullback to pick it off as he speeds by on his course. The ball should be offered waist-high and then laid softly and with extreme care into the pocket made by the fullback's hands and arms. Gentleness is the watchword in this ball exchange. No fake is required, just conservative ball-handling.

The play is extremely fast, but the quarterback must not hurry or act in haste. He must move fast and deliberately, but not hurry, or his ball-handling responsibility will also reflect haste. The fullback and quarterback should practice as a team to perfect the delicate exchange. The height at which the ball is offered is vitally important and the quarterback must adjust that level to the fullback's running style as he hits the line.

After handing off the ball to the fullback, the QB drops back as if he were going to pass. This backfield action lends itself ideally to a spot pass as the driving fullback holds the linebacker's attention, making their zones open to a short pass.

Fullback

The fullback is positioned directly behind the ball and he normally varies his depth according to the play that has been called, maintaining a standard depth of 4 yards from the line of scrimmage. He uses a three-point stance and the depth is measured from his feet, not his hand, when he is in the ready-to-go position.

By constant drilling with the quarterback and pulling guards in the quick trap drill, the fullback determines exactly how shallow he can align himself and make 31 Trap a truly precise play. His objective in setting his depth is to crowd the ball as much as possible and not run into his pulling guard, although running right off his tail through the hole made by the trap block.

We have discovered that most fullbacks move forward to a depth of 3½ yards to make the quick trap really fast. When running behind our smallest guard, 173-pound Randy Cubero, who was extremely fast (he had to be!), our 1958 fullback, Steve Gallios, used to cheat up to 2½ yards and challenge Randy to try to beat him to the hole! Talk about a quick opener! 31 Trap was a streak of lightning that year, and a wonderful change of pace in the attack.

Having lined up at his predetermined depth, the fullback's next job is to take a glance at the defensive alignment to see if it is even or odd. The quickest method, of course, is to determine if there is a lineman head-up on the center. If so, the fullback knows that he must veer his course 45 degrees immediately after getting the ball from the quarterback. In this case, the change of course would be to the left where the 31 Trap point of attack is set.

Against an odd defense, the quarterback must really be certain to pivot out flat because of the veer in the fullback's course after ball exchange. Should the center be uncovered, the fullback would charge straight ahead right over the ball, with no veer in his direction as the blocking pattern would be a scissors move between the center and right guard. (This even defensive alignment will be used as an example in the halfback quick trap to be detailed next.)

On the snap of the ball, the fullback sprints out of his stance and immediately forms the pocket for the ball by raising his left elbow up and placing his right hand in a palm-up position to trap the ball. With head and eyes up, the fullback grasps the ball and follows directly on the tail of the guard, bursting into the alley formed by the angle blocks and the key trap block as executed by the right guard. After getting past the linebackers, the fullback is advised to break directly downfield toward the goal posts. This direction has provided the most yardage and seems to take fullest advantage of the downfield blocking pattern.

Left Halfback

From his wingback position, the left halfback goes in motion early as a decoy with an aiming point one yard behind the fullback.

Right Halfback

Should the right halfback be aligned (as in this description) as a slotback, he releases on the snap count and blocks the near safety man in the downfield pattern. Should he line up in a normal halfback spot, the right halfback would run laterally to his left, behind the fullback and in front of the quarterback who is dropping back to fake a pass. The quarterback would then fake to him as in the pattern for the crossbuck that complements 31 Trap.

Left End

Rule: *Nearest linebacker.* The shortside end fires out and uses a high shoulder block on the nearest linebacker. He usually has a good angle to handle the linebacker but must really explode off the line in order to beat his own fullback to the point of attack. He should clear to the inside unless his path in front of the defender is completely blocked. Going behind the lineman across from him uses too much time in this quick-hitter.

Left Guard

Rule: *Man over center, middle linebacker; if none, pull and trap first man to outside.* In this case, there is a man over center and so the left guard blocks him. The shortside guard aims at the near hip of his target, normally executing a right shoulder block to drive the defender down the line. His target has usually been set up for the right shoulder block because of the center's charge to the right. Should there be no opponent covered off on the center, the left guard would execute the third phase of his rule for 31 Trap. This situation would arise if the defense were using a wide tackle six, even defense. Then the left guard would pull and turn out to his outside, which would serve as an influence move on the victim of the trap.

Center

Rule: *Block away.* In carrying out his rule, the center blocks the first man away from him at the point of attack, whether that man be on or off the line of scrimmage. To block a linebacker, the center executes a high shoulder block to knock the defender off balance. The center's rule is sometimes altered to handle a particular tough opponent, which would mean that a double team block must be put upon the man head-up on center. In such a situation, the center would be the post man, stopping the charge of the defender, while the left guard drove him down the line. It has been found, however, that the single angle blocks serve very well for the quick traps because of the fast timing involved.

Right Guard

Rule: *Pull and trap first man past the center.* The fundamental coaching points in the quick trap technique are quickness, balance and hitting on the rise. The guard is not concerned with whether or not the center will be in his path, but rather is confident, as a result of constant drilling, that the center will fire out and be out of the way immediately. The guard thrusts his left arm back and to the left to start his pull, while at the same time pushing off his right foot and stepping laterally with his left. These three moves, which are really coordinated into one, literally throw the guard in the direction of his block while giving him excellent balance to charge with power. The step with the left foot must be a short lead move, purely directional in purpose.

The right guard's course takes him at approximately 45 degrees to the line of scrimmage into the blocking zone. He *does not pull laterally,* but goes up into the hole, right over the spot vacated by his center. By following such a course, the guard can make certain to have good trapping position on even the most difficult of opponents to trap—the man who does not charge across the line or the one who reacts quickly to the inside to resist being trapped. The trapper is ready immediately to block any opponent in the zone, and this awareness takes care of red-dogging linebackers or other stunts at the point of attack.

The blocking technique is quite simply a near shoulder block executed underway. In this instance it would be a left shoulder block with the guard's head being placed on the near hip in keeping with the principle of placing the head in the hole between the defender and the ball carrier. The guard uncoils as he makes contact to deliver a sharp blow, hits on the rise from an extremely low charge and continues his leg drive and snappy footwork to move the defender laterally out of the zone. The guard must never hesitate in the attack zone, for to do so would clog up the running alley and the fullback would trip over his own teammate's legs.

Inside Tackle

Rule: *Release*. The inside tackle releases to his inside, always making certain to charge across in front of any opponent aligned in front of him. In so doing, he makes certain that no defender will catch the fullback from behind.

Strong Tackle

Rule: *Release*. The strong tackle releases downfield on a very shallow course in an effort to get in front of this extremely quick play. He most likely will execute a peelback block to avoid being involved in a possible clipping violation.

Spread End

Rule: *Release*. The release rule is standard for the spread end, but he must always endeavor to get over in front of the play. He must also be watching intently the reaction of the secondary defenders in his passing zone as he sets up a good pass route for future use.

THE 40 TRAP

Using the same blocking rules and techniques, this extremely fast play is an excellent semi-counter-play for the shortside belly series. The timing is as rapid as the fullback quick trap and the potential breakaway aspect is greater because the ball carrier's course is straight, with no veer necessary as in the fullback play —and the ball carrier is usually the fastest runner on the team, the left halfback. If he pops clear of the linebackers, he has an excellent opportunity to go all the way because a screen of teammates is available downfield, having released from the long side of the unbalanced line.

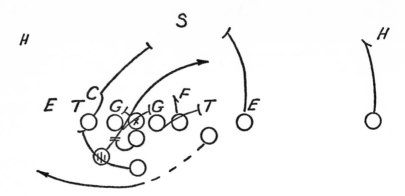

DIAGRAM 46. 40 Trap.

The similarity to the basic shortside belly plays is apparent with the flow being established by the right half's motion toward the short side and the fullback's course as in 37 Belly. Naturally, in order to have the left halfback in normal position as a ball carrier, this play can be run only from peel, or slot, formation, not a double wing alignment.

This play has produced some fine touchdown runs and was the favorite play of one of the Falcon's finest halfbacks, Mike Quinlan. He raced over 60 yards on the quick trap play to score the winning touchdown against a strong and determined Colorado team in 1958.

After pounding off-tackle and outside to establish the running game, 40 Trap is sprung quickly right up the middle in a surprise change of pace stroke.

Quarterback

To start the play pattern, the quarterback reverse pivots on his left foot in much the same manner as the 37 Belly play. However, his footwork is a bit different after the initial move. The variation is relatively minor, but extremely important because of the split-second timing of the ball exchange. The point for the quarterback to remember is that he is not required to reach all the way back to the fullback. The first step in the belly direction by the fullback and the quarterback, plus the fly-back action of the right halfback, gives all the fake required. The remainder of the backfield action effectiveness is all speed and timing.

To assure that the ball exchange will be executed safely, despite the speed with which the ball carrier runs past him, the quarterback must be careful as to where he places his right foot upon completing his reverse pivot. If he pivots around too far, he will be in the way of the onrushing halfback, whose path must be kept clear to provide opportunity for a full speed ahead operation. If he fails to pivot around far enough, he will fail to make connections with the halfback in the ball exchange as the ball carrier will be past him before he can be handed the ball. The recommended course for the quarterback's pivot is about 60 degrees from the line of scrimmage instead of the 45-degree course followed in 37 Belly. This course will give the illusion of the belly play and still permit the QB to complete a reverse pivot handoff to his left halfback without getting in his way as the ball carrier sprints to the right at the spot that the center occupies.

As in the fullback quick trap, the ball exchange responsibility lies solely with the quarterback. Because of the extremely close timing tolerance inherent with 40 Trap, it is recommended that the QB control the ball at all times with both hands. A great deal of centrifugal force is developed in the rapid reverse pivot and he must not lose complete control of the football. He must also concentrate on the proper level of the ball (waist high) because his back is turned toward the left halfback until he completes his pivot. He has only time enough to get a quick glance of the halfback speeding by and has very little opportunity to lay the ball out for the ball carrier. Most of the time, the quarterback must whirl along with the left halfback, placing the ball in the pocket as swiftly and gently as possible under the conditions to complete the ball exchange.

To insure the concentration of the quarterback on the precision hand and footwork, he is not required to do anything else. After the hand-off, he merely protects himself as best he knows how. The play is over as far as he's concerned.

Fullback

Since 40 Trap is a complementary play with the belly series, the fullback must carry out the illusion of a shortside fullback belly play. His course is the standard 37 Belly, quick, slightly rounded, slant at the off-tackle spot. The vital part of his assignment is the very first step. He must explode off the mark instantaneously with the snap count because his first step, and that of the quarterback, constitutes the directional fake of 40 Trap. No other fake is necessary since the play has been set up by constant repetition of the belly play.

Left Halfback

The ball carrier's role in this fast-hitting play requires that the left halfback be extremely careful about his positioning before the ball is snapped.

Most halfbacks will move up to within 2½-3 yards of the line of scrimmage and adjust laterally in toward the center, approximately 2 feet from their normal position behind the shortside end. Any individual adjustment other than these is determined in the same manner that the fullback used in the trapping drill. The objective of the positioning is to be able to hit into the line immediately on the tail of the trapping guard.

The question of ball exchange is not pertinent to the halfback; that problem rests with the quarterback who must spin quicker to make connection with a really fast back. In assuming his correct position for 40 Trap, the left halfback must be certain to face straight ahead in a square alignment so as not to tip the play.

On the snap of the ball, the left halfback sprints full speed at an aiming point that is determined by whether the defensive team is odd or even. If the center is uncovered by a lineman, the left half's straight line target is the football. If there is a lineman head-up on the center, the halfback's course is directed at the center's right foot. In either event, the course is a direct shot through the line of scrimmage with no change in course anticipated until the ball carrier pops into the secondary. At that time he usually will find a good blocking screen to his right and should cut toward that sideline for distance.

Right Halfback

From his slotback position (or wing), the right half flies back in motion ahead of the snap count to give the appearance of a flow play to the left.

Left End

Rule: *Release*. (The rules for "zero" traps are the reverse of "one" traps and so the line assignments will be symmetrical with those outlined for 31 Trap, the fullback quick trap.)

Left Guard

Rule: *Pull and trap the first man past the center*. The shortside guard employs the quick trap technique as detailed for the right guard in 31 Trap. However, in this illustration (Diagram 46), the play is executed against an even-spaced defense, the wide tackle six. The opposition would most likely align itself thus in an effort to counterbalance the shortside attack. This is another reason why 40 Trap is a fine complement to the shortside belly plays, 37 and 29 Belly. The quick trap technique becomes the scissors move for the trapping guard.

In executing the scissors technique, the left guard's initial move requires balance and aggressive power; but it resembles more a rocker step and drive-out than it does a true pulling maneuver. The guard must be ready immediately to make contact and must also charge up into the hole, across the line of scrimmage to dig his target out if necessary.

Center

Rule: *Block away.* The center blocks to his left, away from the target of the trap. His opponent is the man head-up on the pulling guard. That defender will react with the pulling action of the left guard and will be charging laterally into the center. Therefore the center must move quickly to make contact with a left shoulder block on the opponent's near hip, driving hard and fast to remove his feet from the path of the ball carrier. Should the opponent be lined up in the gap between the left guard and center and give every indication of charging hard and low across the line, the center's objective becomes one of stopping penetration. In this situation, a reverse body block is prescribed.

In executing the reverse body block, the center shoots his right forearm and head across in front of the defensive man, aiming for the far hip. He pushes off with the inside of his right foot and makes contact with his right shoulder and with the right side of his body. After making contact, the center works his feet around behind the defender in a crab-like maneuver to maintain blocking pressure, all the while keeping his body between the defender and the trap hole. This move usually requires that the center be on all fours.

Right Guard

Rule: *Man over center, middle linebacker, if none; pull and trap first man to the outside.* In this situation, an evenly spaced alignment with no man over center and no middle linebacker, the right guard pulls and traps the first man to his outside. He would pull in the approved manner and make contact with a right shoulder block. The pulling motion, plus a little wider initial spacing, helps to influence the defender who will be trapped by being drawn further to the outside. This reaction automatically makes the hole at the line of scrimmage wider, even before the block is executed by the trapping guard.

Inside Tackle

Rule: *Nearest linebacker.* The tackle's man is directly opposite him. He charges directly at him to make contact high on the chest with a shoulder block. An effort should be made to place the head between the linebacker and the ball carrier. Should the linebacker tend to pursue immediately into the hole over center, the inside tackle should lead him and throw his body in front of him to cut him down before he reaches the point of attack.

Strong Tackle

Rule: *Release.* This tackle charges directly downfield to block the near safety man. His block is the vital key to springing the ball carrier because the halfback's course is directly at the safety man. The runner will cut behind the block thrown by the strong tackle whose technique usually is the rolling body block.

Spread End

Rule: *Release.* In releasing on 40 Trap, the right end pushes his man straight back and then blocks him, not an opponent to his inside. Thus, the spread end forms the end man in the blocking screen for the left halfback, who is veering toward the side line and long yardage.

16

The Counter and Long Traps

A COMPANION PLAY for the fullback quick trap is the halfback counter trap. Since the fullback quick trap selected for detailed explanation before was 31 Trap, the counter trap to be outlined briefly is 27 counter trap. The backfield action is designed to present virtually the same pattern to the defensive team as they saw in 31 Trap. The object is to freeze the defense with the threat of the fullback quick-opener, and then strike off-tackle with the halfback following the trapping guard as he carries out his long trap technique against the second lineman past the center. The basic impact of the play action is that of a crossback.

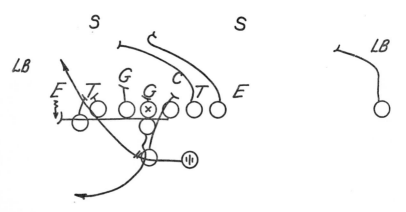

DIAGRAM 47.   27 Counter Trap.

27 COUNTER TRAP

Quarterback

The play action starts with the quarterback reverse pivoting on his left foot, just as he does in 31 Trap. His footwork differs, however, from that quick-hitting play in that he need not whirl around as far. His right foot is planted far enough around in the pivot to insure clearance for the fullback. From that first step on, the quarterback moves straight back away from the line of scrimmage because he wants to intercept the lateral course of the right halfback as soon as possible.

As the fullback drives past, the quarterback fakes to him with his left hand while holding the ball in his right. As the QB places his left foot in his second step, he extends the ball to the pocket formed by the right halfback, who is the ball carrier for 27 counter trap. After the exchange has been completed, the quarterback continues on a bootleg course behind the path of the ball carrier to set up a potential pass pattern from this fine crossbuck action.

Fullback

The fullback drives straight ahead on the snap of the ball, forming a pocket for the exchange fake from the quarterback. After receiving the hand fake from the QB, the fullback veers to his *right* to fill the hole made when the right guard pulled to execute his long trap block. So, instead of following the guard as in 31 Trap, the fullback's course is opposite as he serves as a fill blocker to prevent penetration of defenders through the hole.

Right Halfback

The right halfback lines up in his regular halfback position as regards lateral distance from the fullback; but he cheats back to 4 yards of depth so as to provide a better running angle on this play. His regular stance has him in excellent position to run left as he has his left foot back and his left hand down on the turf for balance. He thus starts laterally to his left merely by an opening directional lead step with his left foot.

On his next step, he forms the ball pocket with his right elbow raised. By the time he has planted his left foot again in the third step, he has the ball and then drives at the off-tackle hole behind the key block of the pulling guard. He should aim as close as possible to the double team power block, for there he is certain to find the most daylight running room.

Left Halfback

The left halfback, set in his wingback position, is the drive blocker of the double team power block at the point of attack.

Left End

Rule: *Inside, on* (*double team*). The shortside end becomes the post blocker for the wingback against the defense as aligned in the diagram for 27 Counter Trap.

Left Guard

Rule: *Inside, on.* The shortside guard blocks straight ahead. If his opponent is a lineman he uses a shoulder block, making certain not to position-step until after making contact with his helmet and shoulder pad. A high shoulder block is used against a linebacker.

Center

Rule: *On, away.* With an opponent lined up directly across from him, the center has no choice except to block him with a shoulder block, placing his head between the defender and the path of the ball carrier. Should he be uncovered, the center would block away from the point of attack using a reverse body block to prevent penetration.

Right Guard

Rule: *Pull to left and block first man outside wingback.* The guard's pulling technique is similar to the quick trap as far as getting underway is concerned. But, since he is executing the long trap, he runs parallel to the line of scrimmage, one foot behind his own linemen's feet to avoid being tripped up by an errant foot. As he approaches the contact point, the right guard gathers his strength in a dipping move so that he can uncoil and strike a powerful blow from below. He is ready to veer into the line to dig out a defender who did not come across; but he normally gets good position for the inside-out left shoulder block on the defensive end.

Should there be no space for a good shoulder block because of a fine defensive reaction by the end, the pulling guard throws a body block to tie up the defender, realizing that the ball carrier will then veer to the outside to find new daylight running room.

Inside Tackle

Rule: *On, release.* The inside tackle bumps, keeping contact with a shoulder block for one count, then releases downfield.

Strong Tackle

Rule: *Release.* It is difficult to get in front of this play to form an adequate downfield screen; but the strong tackle should hustle across-field in case the ball carrier should cut back.

Spread End

Rule: *Release.* 27 Counter Trap is the type of play on which the spread end should vary his lateral spacing to determine what advantage can be acquired. A move to tighter spacing is indicated, which would let him know if the secondary defender is conscious of him as a man-for-man opponent, or whether he is playing the field area in a zone fashion of secondary defense.

44 BACK TRAP

The example from the Flexible T repertoire to be detailed as the long trap play to the unbalanced strong side of the line is 44 Back Trap. This play also fits in well with the longside belly series and is particularly effective as a weapon to handle a tackle who reacts particularly fast to flow, or who has been difficult to block in the fullback off-tackle plays. The play pattern causes the defensive lineman to fight to the outside and toward the fullback; then suddenly that lineman is blocked from the inside by a pulling guard and another potential ball carrier appears from nowhere to dart through the line of scrimmage. The back trap is a special type of change of pace in that it has two obvious paces built into one play. There is the relatively slow ride at the beginning, which is replaced by the full speed slant aspect of the left halfback driving behind the trap block.

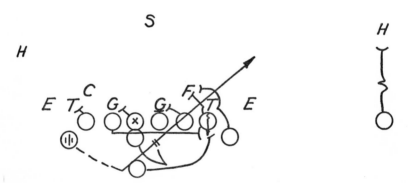

DIAGRAM 48.   44 Back Trap.

Quarterback

The footwork for the quarterback in 44 Back Trap is as complex as any play in the system. It requires a great deal of rehearsal and a quarterback who is well-coordinated with a good sense of rhythm. He reverse pivots as in the longside belly play (36 Belly) and intercepts the fullback on a 45 degree course from the line of scrimmage. He rides the fullback for one quick shuffling step, then withdraws the ball to start the movement which gives the back trap its name, the handing back of the ball to the left halfback.

As he plants his left foot in the shuffle ride along the fullback's course, the quarterback withdraws the ball and pivots on his left foot turning back toward the approaching left halfback. At this point, the QB is faced exactly *away* from the line of scrimmage and he twists his trunk almost 90 degrees further to make certain of the ball exchange to the slanting halfback. After handing off the ball, the QB drops back behind the original position of the strong tackle to set up the play-action pass pattern of the series.

Fullback

The fullback starts laterally, under control, for three steps in the 36 Belly pattern before turning toward the line and making the ball pocket for a ride from his quarterback. His aiming point after the ride is just outside of the opponent to be trapped. This man will usually be found opposite the strong tackle or slightly to his outside. The fullback's intention is to help draw that defender to the outside and thus set him up for a devastating trap block from the blind side.

Left Halfback

The potential ball carrier, the left halfback, lines up as a wingback and has a delicate timing responsibility. He should start in motion early, be under complete control, and then slant full speed behind the trapping guard so as to hit the line with authority. But he must be certain to make connections with the quarterback to insure a good ball exchange. Just as the quarterback's moves require a great deal of practice, the halfback must drill with him often to master the pattern.

The left halfback's fly-back course is the same as usual, one yard behind the fullback, but he must run more under control than usual, perhaps at ½ speed. After his third step he plants his right foot and drives in a slant course directly at the hole and behind the pulling guard. He makes the ball pocket, takes the ball, and upon springing past the linebackers, his most productive course is a veer toward the right sideline behind the downfield blocking screen of the right halfback and spread end.

Right Halfback

Set as the right wingback in a double wing right formation, the right halfback fakes at the defensive man across from him in an effort to influence him so that he will be blocked in. The halfback may actually make contact, but he must be sure not to become entangled or delayed more than one count because he has a vital responsibility downfield. He is assigned to block the near safety man which he does with a rolling body block.

Left End

Rule: *Inside, on, outside.* The off-side end would normally release on a play to the opposite side; but it has been found that penetration pursuit from behind can stop the 44 Back Trap before it reaches the line of scrimmage. Therefore, the left end's assignment is to block at the line of scrimmage, in a semi-passive manner, to prevent pursuit of the left halfback.

Left Guard

Rule: *Pull to the right and trap the second lineman past center.* The guard is advised that his target usually will be aligned opposite the strong tackle position. He pulls and executes the long trap technique, making certain to hit from a low posture, on the rise, with a crisp right shoulder block. Placing his head between the target defender and the running alley for the ball carrier, the left guard will spring the ball carrier for a potential long gaining play.

Center

Rule: *On, away.* Against the wide tackle six, even spacing, the center would execute the "away" part of his rule. A near shoulder block or a reverse body block will permit him to carry out his assignment and prevent pursuit penetration.

Right Guard

Rule: *Inside, on, (double team).* The right guard becomes the post man in the all-important double team power block. A double team block at the point of attack is advisable in a long trap because of the timing required before the ball carrier reaches the hole. The fast-hitting time of a quick trap does not require a double team block, but the defender must be pinned down completely in a long trap; thus the power block is employed as a basic technique.

Inside Tackle

Rule: *Down, inside (double team).* The inside blocks "down" as the drive man of the double team. The term "down" is used to differentiate from inside because it means that he would leave a man "on" him to help to his inside. In Diagram

48, the linebacker is actually "on" the inside tackle, but he is disregarded to help form the necessary double block.

Strong Tackle

Rule: *Nearest linebacker.* The strong tackle blocks the nearest linebacker after bumping the lineman across from him. The technique is a high shoulder block with foot positioning applied after contact is made with helmet and shoulder pads.

Spread End

Rule: *Release and block nearest man in secondary.* The right end releases directly at the back covered off on him. He should coast a few steps, then run full speed through the man with a rolling block. The relaxed approach allows time for the ball carrier to burst through the line and then use the end's block as a screen as he cuts toward the sideline.

44 BACK TRAP PASS

The action of the rather complex pattern of 44 Back Trap lends itself very well to a scoring-type pass play. The time taken to complete the fake of the backs permits the two receivers to drive deep into the secondary and a long completion is a real possibility.

Quarterback

He completes the ride fake with the fullback, the back trap fake with the left halfback, and then drops back to a depth of 8 yards before setting up to throw the pass. The ball should be hidden on his left hip after the back trap fake to the halfback, and the quarterback's head and eyes, plus his empty right hand, follow the path of the halfback into the hole.

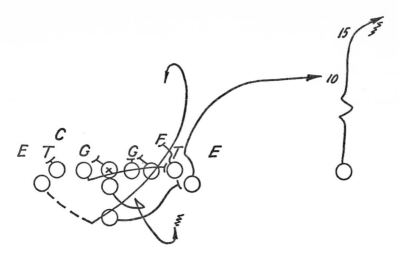

DIAGRAM 49. 44 Back Trap Pass.

Fullback

After completing his belly ride fake with the quarterback, the fullback becomes a part of the pass protection. He is especially responsible for the area vacated by the right wingback and is outside-conscious.

Left Halfback

He runs the exact course through the line of scrimmage as he does in 44 Back Trap. Should the guard's trap block spring him, the left halfback runs a pass route to an open spot down the short middle zone of the defensive secondary. His presence in the pass pattern is not relied upon; but should he get free, he can be an important safety valve for the quarterback.

Right Halfback

From his wingback position, the right halfback can influence-bump the lineman across from him before running his pass route. The delay involved is accepted because the halfback is to run the short half of the pass pattern and will not be the prime receiver for the quarterback. After releasing, the right halfback pushes straight downfield for 8 to 10 yards and then breaks sharply toward the right sideline.

Spread End

The widely spaced right end is the No. 1 target for the passer. He releases directly at his defender, running under control and gathering as if to block the man. As soon as the defender reacts to the simulated block and the play-action in the backfield, the spread end bursts forward at full speed bending his course slightly to the right in a flag route. He should take the lofted pass from his quarterback over his right shoulder.

The entire line blocks aggressively just as they do in 44 Back Trap, even to the double team power block and the pulling long trap by the left guard. The left end executes his block in a more conservative fashion in order to assure the quarterback of ample time to get the pass away without quick pressure from the rear. Despite the fact that 44 Back Trap Pass is a long pattern and its intent is a touchdown, the complex faking pattern takes time, and the quarterback can usually throw the ball as soon as he is set. The release of the ball at this time makes a very effective pattern because the spread end is usually just speeding into the clear at that instant.

Variation to Make Use of "Near Trap" Blocking

"Near trap" blocking, in which the trap is executed by the nearest guard to the point of attack instead of the guard pulling from the far side of center, is a profitable variation. The near trap technique is especially effective against a gap defense, the outside-shaded positioning of the 4-5 or 6-3 defense, or the inside tackle adjustment of the 5-4 defense, commonly known as the Eagle defense.

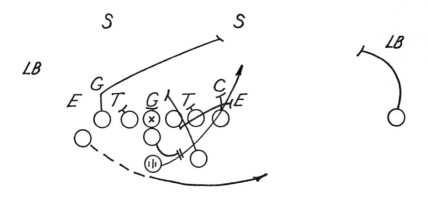

DIAGRAM 50.   36 Belly Pull.

The play in the Flexible T offense that lends itself best to the use of the near trap technique is the fullback belly play. The diagram illustrates 36 Belly with the added descriptive term "pull." The term means just that to the onside guard, who will automatically pull and trap the first man outside his strong tackle. The onside halfback, if any, will fill the hole vacated by the guard to seal off penetration and help freeze the reaction of the defense.

The inside tackle's rule is to block down to his inside, as is the rule for the strong tackle. These rules, plus the pulling technique, give 36 Belly (pull) good angle blocks—cross-action which provides excellent strength at the point of attack and still permits a quick-hitting play. When 36 Belly (pull) is called, the fullback runs a quicker pattern, almost an off-tackle slant course, and the quarterback does not have opportunity for much of a ride effect.

17

Flexible T Drive Series

THE DRIVE SERIES is the most powerful one in the Flexible T offense. It generates its power from the massed formations and the ample use of power blocks. The adjective "drive" is most descriptive as everyone on the attack is made conscious of the surging power desired in the series, and they seem to put out an extra spurt of energy to drive back the defensive team and control the line of scrimmage.

An Effective Game-Opening Play

The drive series is an excellent one from which the quarterback can select a play to start a game because the ball-handling is simple, the blocking assignments are straight ahead, and everyone on the team makes good hard contact. Thus, a play like 23 Drive serves well as a "relaxisizer" to remove all signs of nervous energy from a team at the start of a game. The jitters and "butterflies-in-the-stomach" feeling will be quickly dispersed after one massed drive play wherein every attacking player can unload on an opponent, then be ready to settle down to an alert, but relaxed, football game.

Excellent for Consistent Short-Yardage Gains

The four running plays of the drive series (one halfback play to each side of the unbalanced line and one fullback play to each side) have been the most consistently productive plays in the entire offense. Seldom do these drive plays break away for long touchdown runs, but they add a consistency to the attack which assures maintaining possession.

The series' running plays have averaged 3.7 yards per try and their consistency hovers around 85 per cent, a fine average indeed. Very seldom do these plays fail to gain their 2-3 yards, even under most difficult short yardage and goal line situations. There is very little opportunity for the defense to penetrate into the backfield because of the massed straight-ahead aspect of the drive plays. Much of the series' success can be attributed to the double team blocks, sometimes two at the point of attack where the opponents are definitely outnumbered.

When directed at the short side of the unbalanced line, the halfback drive play, 23 Drive, mounts two double team blocks where the opposing team has fewest men. The double team blocks pierce the defense and the majority of the opponents are out of it because they are aligned to the long side. The ball carriers are instructed that the play will be most productive when the massed forces are aimed directly at a linebacker. It is believed that more daylight for running room will open up and the degree of control of the line of scrimmage will also be at a maximum. The linebackers, being back off the line, and in an upright stance, are less capable of withstanding a frontal attack such as the drive series mounts.

The basic play of the series is the halfback play to the short side. It has the elements of an inside belly play; but as taught in the Flexible T, there is absolutely no belly ride to the fullback as the play is intended to be a powerful quick-hitter— finesse is not a desired fundamental. The play, 23 Drive, is a second-back-through action in the backfield and therefore does have some freezing effect upon the linemen near the point of attack.

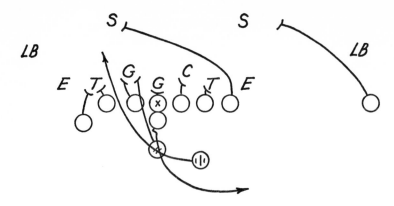

DIAGRAM 51.   23 Drive.

23 DRIVE

Quarterback

The faking involved in 23 Drive is virtually achieved 100 per cent by the course of the fullback and is not the result of any special sleight-of-hand ball-handling by the quarterback. Without any thought of faking, the quarterback pivots back on his right foot with the ball firmly in both hands. His first step turns him completely around with his back to the line of scrimmage. The fullback runs extremely close to him and so the quarterback holds the ball firmly to thwart a fumble should the FB brush up against him. The ball is not offered to the fullback, although he does fake reception at this time.

The quarterback takes a second shorter step, with no hesitation, and hands the ball off to the right halfback who is driving hard in a circular course toward the point of attack. The QB momentarily comes to a halt at the ball exchange point so as to allow the halfback access to the point of attack in the general zone of the 3 hole, which is over the guard or slightly to his outside.

Should the quarterback push the ball carrier deep he would

be unable to turn the corner at full speed, nor would he be able to hit any daylight that might appear to his inside. Thus, to allow a full speed corner and to afford the right halfback the chance to hit the line in a perpendicular fashion, the quarterback must stay in a relatively shallow spot behind the center until after the halfback is past. Then the quarterback rolls out away from the play-action to set up the bootleg pass that is an integral part of the drive series.

Fullback

The fullback lines up about a foot or so closer to the ball than usual, placing himself about $3\frac{1}{2}$ yards deep. This position will permit the fast timing of 23 Drive and will also make the fullback a more effective blocking partner with his left guard, in one of the drive's two double team power blocks. The fullback is the only faker in the pattern. He aims at the inside foot of his left guard who has spaced 2 feet from the center.

Driving at his target, the fullback forms a ball pocket with his right elbow up and, as he speeds by the quarterback, he lowers his inside shoulder as if carrying the ball. That's his faking responsibility. Now for his blocking role. With head and eyes up, the FB takes dead aim on the linebacker who by this time has been straightened up and preoccupied by the shoulder block of the left guard. The fullback drives into the linebacker with a high left shoulder block to complete the double team, as the guard has attacked with a right shoulder block. The partners' objective is to drive the linebacker straight back as far as possible.

Right Halfback

The ball-carrying right halfback must position himself precisely if he is to be able to round the corner at full speed and hit the daylight at the line of scrimmage at a 90 degree angle.

To do this, he cheats back to about a foot *deeper* than the fullback and a foot closer to him laterally than is normal. On the snap count, the halfback starts a full speed circular course to the point of attack, following just a shade to the outside of the fullback's course. The aiming point is the left foot of the left guard whereas the fullback's was the right foot. After receiving the ball from the quarterback (right elbow raised) the halfback seeks the daylight, usually running just to the outside of the double team block on the linebacker.

Left Halfback

Rule: *Inside, on (double team)*. The left halfback, from his wingback position, blocks as the drive man in the double team with the left end. Their objective is to control the line of scrimmage and drive their man straight back.

Left End

Rule: *Inside, on (double team)*. The shortside end serves as the post man in the double team block with the wingback. He stops the defender's charge and then drives him back off the line.

Left Guard

Rule: *Inside, on (double team)*. The shortside guard's rule is simple, but it requires detailed explanation because his assignment is to be carried out in conjunction with the fullback.

Normally, the staff would not be concerned as to which shoulder a lineman blocked; but in this assignment, the guard must block with his right shoulder so as to allow blocking room for the fullback in the double team.

Center

Rule: *On, away*. The center normally will have a lineman or linebackers directly upon him. He must drive straight ahead and tie up his opponent by constant leg drive.

Right Guard

Rule: *Inside, on.* Fire out straight ahead and scramble after initial shoulder block contact.

Inside Tackle

Rule: *Inside, on, release.* The inside tackle, although not near the point of attack, should also fire out to block the nearest opponent, driving him back off the line as far as possible.

Strong Tackle

Rule: *Release.*

Spread End

Rule: *Release.*

The same basic pattern is used for the fullback drive play to the short side in the event that a quick straight-ahead power play is required. Sometimes, the second-back-through timing of 23 Drive meets too quick a reaction by the defense. The opponents have been known to ignore the fullback in the pattern, realizing that he is a lead blocker, so a change-up is effective and merely requires giving the ball to the fullback and faking to the halfback as he comes by.

As with all of the basic plays in the Flexible T attack, the drive plays can be run to the long or short sides of the unbalanced line as well as from the line left or line right formations. Rather than detail the same (42 Drive) play when it is run to the right, a blocking variation will be described for the long-side drive play, and it is given the name 42 Turn Out.

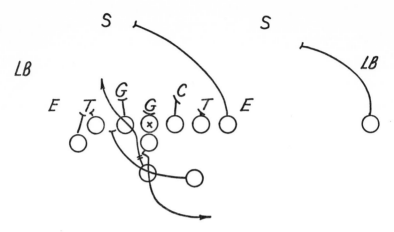

DIAGRAM 52.   33 Drive.

42 TURN OUT

The backfield action pattern is exactly the same as in the drive play but the object of the blocking is to present a new problem of angle blocks and influence to the defenders. Expecting the power treatment of the drive play will set the opponents up for angle blocks in much the same manner that trap blocking does.

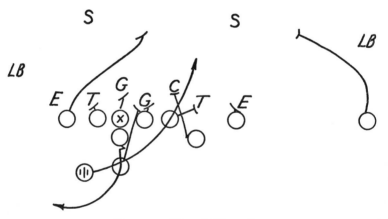

DIAGRAM 53.   42 Turn Out.

This play, too, is designed to strike directly at a linebacker with authority. It is believed that the turn-out style of blocking at the attack point provides much more daylight running room than the normal drive blocking would. Having spaced the defense thin at the intended hole, the angle block by the inside tackle tends to hold the spacing thus gained until the ball carrier gets through. The cross-block aspect of the slotback driving at the linebacker from behind the lateral charge of his inside tackle is quite effective. The slotback can develop a greater amount of power, too, because he has a running start for his block.

The off-side blocking rules remain the same for the turnout as for the off-side linemen in the drive series plays.

Right Guard

The longside guard has the same role of a double team partner with the fullback, but he now must execute his block on an opposing lineman instead of a linebacker. (See Diagram 53.) He fires low and hard into his opponent, making contact with his helmet, then slipping immediately to a left shoulder block. He must make certain to move his feet around to the right quickly to allow room for the fullback who will complete the double team block with a right shoulder technique.

Inside Tackle

Rule: *Turn out and block first man to outside.* This rule means that the tackle must leave a man who is aligned on him (in this instance, a linebacker) and block the next man he encounters to his outside. The turn-out block is a shoulder block which generates a lot of power because it is a surprise move and contact is made from the side, where the opponent offers least resistance to being moved.

Strong Tackle

Rule: *On, outside.* The strong tackle merely keeps his man busily tied up. He does not have to move him because the slot spacing has already accomplished that purpose. His opponent is normally 2-men removed from the point of attack and is not an immediate obstacle to be removed.

Spread End

Rule: *Release, and block in.*

Right Halfback

Rule: *Drop stop and block second man from center.* The slot man drops back on his inside foot to improve his clear path behind the inside tackle, who is turning out. He has also cheated in about a foot from his normal lateral position as the slot man. The drop, or rocker, step gives the proper timing to the blocking pattern, too, as the right halfback can be free to charge full speed ahead at his target. In this example, the target is a linebacker, but it might very well be a lineman. Should his opponent be a lineman, the slot-back's block becomes an outside-in trap, which is also a fine change of technique to employ against a bothersome defender.

42 DRIVE PASS

The drive series does not include a counter-play because the objective is massed, straight-ahead power. The change of pace built into the series takes the form of giving the ball to the first back through (33-32 drive), or in changing the style of blocking at the point of attack. However, the series does include a most productive play-action pass pattern which has proved to be extremely effective and has produced more touchdowns than any other play in the entire system. That play in 42 Drive Pass.

The success of the play in producing long gaining scores can be attributed to the excellent action in the backfield pattern and the fact that the drive series plays are established in the minds of the defense as being massed ground-gaining power plays.

Upon seeing the start of the drive action in the backfield, the defensive team apparently assumes that a straight-ahead running play is forming. There is also something to the theory that a double fake in an action pass play is a most effective maneuver. 42 Drive Pass has that aspect in that the quarterback does not indicate a pass play until both the fullback and left halfback have driven by him in the action pattern. Even then he bootlegs a step or two before planting his feet to throw the pass.

The actual pass pattern used with 42 Drive Pass is an excellent one, too. Even should the secondary defenders expect the pass and react correctly, one of the receivers usually is open. Therefore, an excellent backfield action, a mental impression

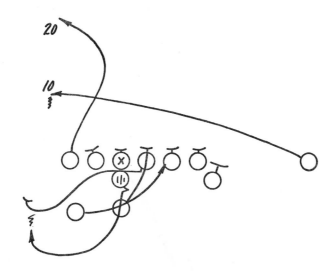

DIAGRAM 54.   42 Drive Pass.

of a running play, and a good 2-man pattern combine to make an excellent scoring play.

Linemen

The entire line, except the ends who run the pass routes, and the right guard who has a special job, block aggressively on this play. The term "aggressive" is not entirely accurate, for in our phraseology, aggressive, for pass protection, involves a definite amount of control. The linemen should charge forward for one step, but then recover after initial contact to keep their opponent from crossing into the backfield and rushing the passer. The object is to show a running play on the snap count and then carry out pass protection responsibility thereafter. Controlled aggressiveness is a more accurate description of their blocking technique.

Right Guard

The right guard has a special job. He is the personal protector for the passer and he must pull to the left, or toward the short side, to acquire position to protect his quarterback. The play-action and bootleg maneuver by the quarterback are not enough of a guarantee that the passer can get the pass away. Because the short side of the unbalanced line places the outside defender closer to the passer than does a balanced alignment, the quarterback requires a personal protector. The longside guard performs that function.

Due to the concentrated play action, the fact that the right guard pulls out of the line, away from the point of attack, is not a giveaway. The only defenders who might be wary that a surprise move is coming are the linemen in the immediate vicinity of the pulling guard. However, they cannot afford to leave their primary area since the backfield action is directed right at them. The right guard pulls to his left using the basic pulling technique, but making absolutely certain to stay very close to the line of scrimmage for two steps in order to clear the quarterback, who does not immediately gain depth in the drive fake.

The guard takes a directional step with his left foot, then one full step with his right before veering away from the line at about a 45 degree angle to acquire depth. He should aim to be 4-5 yards deep and outside of his own left end. The guard should attempt to set up in a good protective stance, facing slightly to the outside to pass-block for the quarterback. He should also be ready, immediately after pulling, to throw a cross body block in the event that the defensive end has penetrated deep and fast into the backfield. Feeling no pressure, the guard should swing his vision from left to right to pick up any onrushing defender. Finally, he must be ready to lead the quarterback around the end as a personal interferer should the passer find all receivers covered and his path open to run. In such an event, the quarterback would shout, "Go!"

Quarterback

The quarterback pivots back on his left foot, permitting the fullback to drive by. Then he places the ball in his right hand only, holding it firmly on his hip as he fakes to the left halfback driving by on course. The fake to the halfback is the real one which should cement the reaction of the defensive secondary that a running play is in progress.

The quarterback puts his empty left hand into the pocket formed by the halfback and then follows his progress with his head and eyes. The QB must hesitate at this point, really putting on an act, fully cognizant that he is protected to the rear by his pulling right guard. Having completed a very deliberate fake of 42 Drive, the quarterback quickly continues on a rounded course to set up 7 yards deep behind his own left end.

He plants his feet firmly and throws a pass. His primary target is the left end who is the deep man; but the right end crossing over shallow is also in the line of vision. Should the defense drop off to defend the pass, the quarterback will have the option to run with the ball, using an audible signal to his personal protector and turning left end.

Fullback

The fullback runs the drive course at the inside foot of his right guard, faking as if getting the ball, then filling as a blocker in the hole vacated by the pulling guard.

Left Halfback

Runs the 42 Drive course and slams into the line as if running with the ball.

Right Halfback

Blocks aggressively as in the running play.

Left End

As the primary and deep pass receiver, the shortside end spaces comfortably to make certain he can clear the line quickly. His route is run completely as a speed break to get necessary depth. He sprints at the near safety as if to block him. At a depth of 10 yards, he breaks out and away from the safety man on a long flag route. His course will be about 30 degrees to the left of straight down the field and he should catch a soft lofted ball around 20-25 yards deep. His route is the touchdown one, but he must be careful not to flatten out too much in the break. If he cuts too sharply from his downfield course and toward the sidelines, there is a danger that the defensive right corner linebacker or defensive right halfback will drop back and break up the pass.

Spread End

The spread end adjusts in laterally to his medium spacing of 8-10 yards to be best positioned to start his pattern, which places him in the opposite flat when the ball is thrown. He should run a straight-line fast course, just behind the linebacker to end up about 8-10 yards deep in the opposite flat. His course at that time is similar to the shallow man running a sideline break pattern. He is an excellent secondary target for the quarterback, especially if the side secondary defenders have dropped back to cover the dangerous deep receiver from the short side of the line.

18

The Possession Passing Attack

THE FLEXIBLE T used by the Falcons at the Air Force Academy has given the system and the Academy football team the reputation of being very air-minded. It is only fitting and proper that the team representing the U. S. Air Force put the football into the air quite often. Indeed, the Falcons have thrown a great many passes and have adopted somewhat of a wide open approach to offensive football. The attack has averaged 25 passes per game with a completion record of exactly 50 per cent, and the average gain per completion just over 10 yards. The passing reputation naturally came also because of the remarkable individual records established by Richie Mayo during the 1958-59-60 seasons. Richie completed 316 passes during his career to rank sixth among all-time collegiate passers. He had single game marks of 53 attempts and 28 completions. Quite an air arm for the air service, the U.S. Air Force!

ROLE OF PASSING IN OVER-ALL OFFENSE

However, the offense is thought of by the staff as being an integrated one. That is, an attack system in which the forward pass plays a definite role, but is not the prime mover. The forward pass is considered an integral part of the offense and should be used just as any other play in the system. The ground game has to be established first, after which the pass plays can readily be integrated into the over-all attack. The two phases of offensive football complement each other nicely but a proper balance must be maintained or the effectiveness of each is lost.

To run the ball all the time is to invite the defensive team to mass close to the line of scrimmage in an effort to counter ground strength. To pass all of the time is to invite deployment off the line. It is believed that the integrated run-and-pass offense, using the ground attack as the fundamental strength, serves best to pose problems to the opponent on defense. They must be ready for either a pass or a run on any given down, any place on the field.

Passing Game Must Be Constant Threat

This last sentence spells out one phase of the basic philosophy of the passing game in the Flexible T offense—throw the ball anytime at any place on the field. The forward pass must be used just as any other play in the repertoire or it will lose much of its effectiveness as a weapon. The defense, if expecting a pass, can defend against it adequately. The pass must be integrated into the attack, and the attacking team must never be *afraid* to throw the ball. Complete confidence in the forward pass is a prerequisite for success in passing.

The passer himself is usually more than willing to throw the ball. Quarterbacks are a confident breed. The pass receivers delight in having a chance to catch a pass no matter when or where their signal is called. The linemen as a group are the ones who must be convinced that the forward pass can best be used as a tactical weapon if license to throw the ball is complete and unlimited. The coaching staff must sell this approach to the entire team and the line coach must hammer away at the theme in the sense of good salesmanship at every opportunity. In practice scrimmages, the forward pass should be thrown from near both goal lines as well as in the middle of the field. Only by such repetition will the linemen become accustomed to using the pass as every other play in the system is used.

To pass must not be considered a desperation play, or last resort. Teams that are forced to pass are very infrequently successful with the passing game. They do not believe in it; it is an unnatural weapon, to be saved for emergency use only. Passes should be thrown just as a team would execute a run off tackle—naturally and confidently.

What Is Possession Passing?

Not every type of pass play will adapt to the confident, integrated pass attack philosophy as outlined above. The attack through the air lanes offered in the Flexible T system is one that we call "possession passing." This description indicates that the offense wants to hold onto the ball as in the 3½-yard ground attack possession theory. Possession of the football is definitely a part of it, but not by grinding out the yardage 3½ yards per attempt along the ground. Such an approach requires superior manpower strength in general, and use of the massed attack. The forward pass can be used to maintain possession if the type of pass play used is strictly limited and the philosophy adhered to in a disciplined manner.

The 'Spot and Timing' Pass

The basic pass offense built into the integrated attack is the spot-and-timing type aimed at the 8-12 yard depth in the defensive secondary.

The average pass completion gives the offense 10 yards gained and, aiming at a minimum completion record of 50 per cent, the gain per pass attempt figures to be 5 yards. If a team

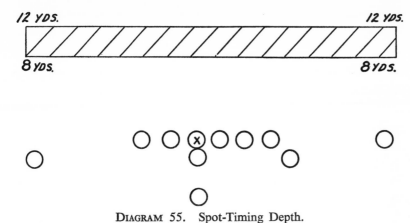

DIAGRAM 55. Spot-Timing Depth.

will accept 5 yards per try on a running play, they should be just as pleased with that same 5 yards, even if garnered by a forward pass.

The inherent danger in throwing a pass, and the reason so many teams do not pass often, is the interception. It has been determined by actual experience that the well-timed, relatively short pass enjoys virtual immunity from interception. It is true that certain zones of the secondary and perimeter defenses are guarded more closely than others. The possession passing at-

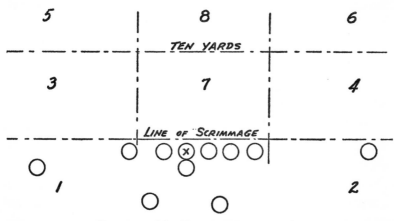

DIAGRAM 56. Zones of Pass Attack.

tack centers its focus upon those zones which are given least emphasis in a standard coverage, thus decreasing again the possibility of interception.

Attacking Passing Zones

This illustration indicates the priority normally assigned to the secondary passing zones. The higher-numbered zones are the most zealously guarded and therefore should be attacked less frequently. To insure completions and avoid interceptions, the zones to be attacked are those assigned the lower numbers. Any ball thrown into zones 1, 2, 3, and 4 should have an excellent chance to find its way to the target. Those flat zones, shallow and deep, are usually unmanned or, at best, occupied by a defender coming from some other position after the action has started.

The middle zones are hardest to hit without danger of interception. Number 8 is toughest because it is the deepest zone and will yield touchdowns if pierced. Zone 7, the short middle, is next toughest because it is usually occupied by more than one defender in the person of linebackers and also requires the passer to throw the ball over outstretched hands and struggling linemen. A ball can easily be tipped or batted up into the air, the most common type of interception.

The priority of zones to the right of the offensive team (2-4-6) is a result of most teams' tendency to attack right-handed. This habit decrees that the defense will place its better defenders in those zones—all the more reason to develop a left-handed attack, which is one of the basic principles of the Flexible T.

How to Increase Pass Completion Average

Having limited the depth of the patterns as well as the zones upon which to concentrate to avoid interceptions, the possession pass attack stresses timing as a means of increasing the completion average. The theory that a well-timed pass, accurately thrown, cannot be knocked down by the defense, is sound. The accuracy is guaranteed as much as possible, even with limited talent as a passer, by forbidding a pass of over 12 yards to be a part of the basic pass offense. By constant practice, any player with average strength as a thrower can develop into a good short-passer. The timing is also a factor that is a result of constant drilling.

Timing as applied in the short-passing offense is a coordinated effort, not just the quarterback's responsibility. Certainly the quarterback, in his vital role as passer, must throw the ball at the proper time. But the receivers must be at the proper spot at that same time, and the pass-protecting linemen must keep their opponents away from the passer at least until that time when the ball is thrown.

Since the patterns are no deeper than 12 yards, the timing can be quick. By the time a receiver has run to his normal spot, the passer has dropped back (or rolled out) to a predetermined spot. In a timing pass play, it is important that the passer be schooled in a set pattern of footwork and not merely drop back and read the field before throwing the ball. Any looseness in this detail will result in the passer's holding the ball too long, waiting for an absolutely clear receiver, and ending up having a long incompletion, an interception, or being thrown for a loss because his protection broke down under the pressure of time.

The Quarterback's Drop Back

The quarterback must drop back to a spot 6-7 yards directly behind the center, plant his feet and step forward as he throws. This footwork gives the linemen a definite spot to protect and the reaction of the defensive rushers in their attempt to get to the passer will be consistent, simplifying the pass blocker's job. It is virtually impossible to protect a passer who will not get set or hold still to be protected.

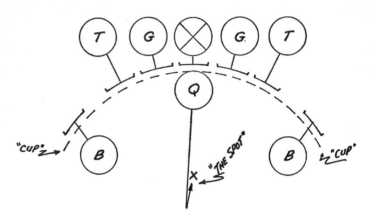

DIAGRAM 57. Cup Pass Protection.

The exact timing sought is for the quarterback to drop back quickly, not hurriedly, to his spot, get set, and throw by a normal count of 6. He should be on the spot by 4, step by 5 and release the ball by 6. The receivers must be on their spots by that same count of 6. The precise timing can be established by drilling with audible counting on the part of a coach for the benefit of both passer and receiver. Later on, the quarterback can cease counting; but the receiver should continue to count to himself until the rhythm is a part of his pass route course. Practicing individual spot passes with the teammate most likely to be in the game is excellent training for both receiver and passer. Getting familiar with the speed of a receiver is invaluable knowledge for the passer who wants to be successful.

The approach thus far described in the possession pass attack involves only the drop-back type of pass technique, although the same timing principle can be applied to roll-out and play-action spot passes. In order to guarantee their responsibility of protecting the passer for at least 6 counts, the linemen (and this can include the shortside end and/or the backs upon occasion) use a modified pass block. In forming the cup protecting the spot from which the passer throws, the protectors are basically responsible for a zone, not a particular man. This style insures that a clean breakthrough will not be made by a powerful charge or a stunt directed at a lone protector. All protectors have the same rule: *inside, on, outside,* except the center who is the middle of the protective cup, and he must block "on," or be a general protector.

Cup Offers Excellent Protection

Maximum protection is the aim of the cup, therefore no effort is made to conceal the intention to pass. Timing and spot patterns are effective even when the defense expects a pass. The linemen drop back forming the cup and assuming a good, strong pass-protective stance. The center drops back one step off the line of scrimmage and flanking protectors drop back deeper as required to form the cup. They also face slightly to the outside while adjusting in laterally to reduce the gaps through which a rusher could penetrate. Their feet constantly "stutter" to maintain balance and to provide for quick recovery. The remainder of the technique involves delivering a shoulder and forearm block (to any rusher coming into their zone), recovering and delivering a second blow. If the rusher continues to pressure the passer, the protector is instructed to cut him down with a body block at this time. He also uses a cross body block as a last resort to erase an opponent escaping to the outside or to cut down an extremely hard-charging and strong rusher immediately.

The effect of the body block is to prevent the rushers from raising their arms and hands up high enough to deflect a pass or to disrupt the clear vision of the quarterback. In a spot-timing pass attack, the protectors can afford to cut their men down sooner than usual because they know that the pass is going to be thrown very soon after the quick 6-count if not exactly on it. Thus, maximum protection for a minimum length of time is achieved.

The same split-timing pass plays can be successfully thrown from play-action fakes as outlined in previous chapters on play series. The controlled aggressive blocks are executed by the protectors. The objective in the play-action passes is to deceive rather than protect. Timing passes can also be thrown from a roll-out or sprint-out technique by the quarterback.

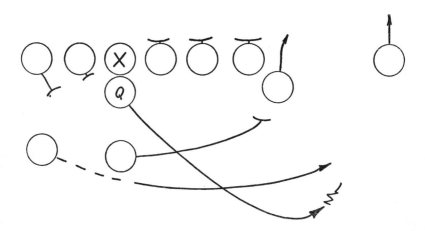

DIAGRAM 58.   Roll Out Technique.

Roll-Out Passes

The roll-out pass play is designed to escape overwhelming rushers from one zone or to exert pass or run pressure upon the flank defenders. Some patterns are most effective when thrown from drop-back while others are best when thrown from the roll-out style of pass attack. The basic difference is the reaction to flow by the defenders who must move their pass defense zones laterally with the flow of the quarterback (because of the ever-present threat of a run around the end) while determining their particular responsibility in the roll-out pass pattern. A drop-back pattern has the result of inducing the defenders to drop back also, thus making them vulnerable to a stop pattern or a 90 degree break to the sideline. The patterns diagrammed as examples will be shown in the preferred formation and style (cup or roll-out).

Since the play-action passes were covered in their respective series, they will not be included in the approach to possession passing. Actually, they are outside the realm because they are not limited as to depth. They have a definite timing aspect, but it is not similar to the short-passing 6-count timing. The play-action passes are designed to produce scores or long gains and not to average 5 yards per attempt as are the possession passes.

Play-action passes are to be called by the quarterback as surprise moves in good tactical situations. They are in the category of "waste-a-down" plays. That implies that position, yards and down, etc., are such that a wasted, non-productive play can be afforded—where the long-shot chance of a score makes the gamble well-advised. Many teams will use a play-action pass, seeking a long gainer by throwing a "home run" pass pattern, when they have a second down and less than 3 yards to gain. Failing to make connections, the team would have a third down and less than 3 yards to be gained. They're still on schedule and normally would be expected to be able to maintain possession of the ball.

Another strategical use of the play-action pass, and not particularly the possession-type, is as a quick-scoring weapon after a surprise possession of the ball in enemy territory. For instance, having gained possession of the ball as a result of a blocked punt or a recovered fumble, the first play called could well be a play-action pass designed to spring loose one deep receiver. The play has a good chance to succeed because the opponents have suffered a drop in morale and may press too hard, reacting unnaturally to the very next play to atone for their mistake or misfortune. 42 Drive Pass (Pg. 174) has contributed such a weapon to the Flexible T.

The Pass Receiver's Course

The technique of the passer has been described in this chapter as well as in Chapter 7. The protection for the passer has been outlined, also. The final part of the possession passing attack to be described involves the receivers. In some instances, the maneuvers described amount to a pass route. A route is an individual receiver's course and it may or may not be a part of a pattern. A pass pattern involves two or more pass receivers following prescribed routes in an effort to break loose one receiver. When running a pass route in a man-for-man situation, the individual receiver is running his own pattern and has to spring himself clear to be a good target. The pass routes and how they fit into the theory of a spot-timing, short-passing attack will be covered first, as the individual courses cover the many ways in which a particular zone may be attacked by one man.

19

Pass Routes and Patterns

THE DIAGRAM that follows shows clearly the basic ways in which one receiver can attack one pass defense zone. In this example the zone is number 3, the left deep flat.

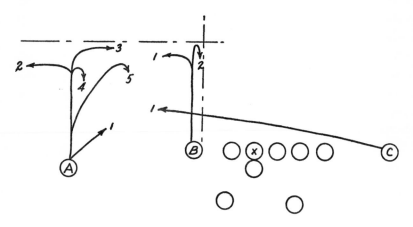

DIAGRAM 59.   Pass Routes in Zone 3.

PASS ROUTES

In the diagram, A is a flanked halfback, B is the shortside end, and C is the longside end. The value of deployment is clearly shown by the preponderance of routes that are available to the flanker (A) as he attacks the zone. The five routes assigned to him place a great burden on the defender assigned to cover him, especially if they are used intelligently and to complement each other in some order, or sequence.

A-1 route is the *look-in* to be thrown with quickest timing possible (as soon as the quarterback can get the ball firmly in his grip) to take advantage of an unguarded spot.

A-2 route is the surest completion in spot passing, the *sideline break,* and it is especially effective to garner that vital first down when a slight comeback angle is built into the route as it nears the sideline.

A-3 route is the *break-in* course, which attacks the center of the zone from the outside. The 90 degree change in course is difficult to defend and the route is an excellent change of pace to the over-used sideline path.

A-4 is the *buttonhook* or *stop* route and is a certain completion if thrown in a one-on-one situation immediately upon the flanker's halt to pushing downfield.

A-5 route is termed the *fish hook* and has been the most efficient of all Flexible T pass routes. Naturally, a great deal of practice time is spent on perfecting the timing and coordination of this route as it is designed for throwing to a spot, but the spot is variable according to the defensive alignment. The flanker must run to an open spot and so position himself to afford the passer a clear path of vision and an unobstructed alley down which to throw the ball. The flanker must avoid any shallow defender (end or linebacker) who may station himself in the line of flight of the ball.

Note: All of the routes described for the flanked halfback are also used, perhaps more so, by the spread end, in attacking Zone 4 to his side of the field.

The flanker attacks the zone from his wide position and the left end (B) can attack it from his normal position, which is inside of the center of the zone.

B-1 route is the standard sideline break.

B-2 is a buttonhook directed at a spot near the borderline of the zone and the short middle zone (7).

The zone may also be attacked from the opposite side of center as is illustrated in the route for the right end (C). He executes a speed break, shallow path that places him in the opposite deep flat. This route is effective because of the direction from which the receiver comes and the speed with which he enters the zone.

Any of the individual pass routes, especially those outlined for the widest man (flanker or spread end) can be called as a one-man pass play and prove effective because of the timing, disciplined route, wide open spaces for maneuvering, and the extra protection given to the quarterback. Non-essential receivers are not deployed, but stay close to the cup protectors and serve in the role of general protectors of a personal nature for the passer.

PASS PATTERNS

Having given the highest praise of efficiency to the *fish hook* pass play, it will be outlined first.

Fish Hook

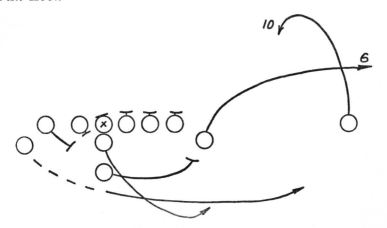

DIAGRAM 60.   Roll Out Fish Hook Pass.

The Fish Hook Pass play is an adaptation of the original "Hook," or stop, pass which was designed especially for the spread end formation and because of the manner in which teams were defensing it. Just about every pass defense includes a man (normally a linebacker) who will drop to the so-called "hook zone" when a forward pass is indicated. This positioning of a defender places him right in the line of flight of a ball thrown to an end running a normal hook, or buttonhook pattern.

The fish hook pattern is designed to accomplish the spot timing of the hook pass. This timing and the fake of going deep, which pushes the deep defenders backward, is a tried, proven and efficient maneuver. But the end must avoid those pesky linebackers in order to catch the ball. Thus the fish hook route. The end runs away from or around the linebacker (as illustrated by the spread end in the diagram). The timing is such that the ball is thrown at about the time the end clears behind the defender and is lost to his vision. The hapless defender is also held, or moved laterally, by the roll-out fake of the quarterback and the fullback of the Falcons' double wing T offense.

Many key completions have been racked up on this simple pass play. It is not designed for long yardage, but is a good gainer for that crucial first down. Eight to 10 yards is an acceptable gain—especially when the completion permits continued possession of the ball.

The fish hook pass was directly responsible for four "must" first downs in the last-minute touchdown drive of the Air Force Academy's victory over a fine Oklahoma State team in 1958. That victory by a 33-29 score was accomplished in the final 9 seconds and allowed the Falcons to finish undefeated and breeze into the Cotton Bowl on New Year's Day.

The heroes of that memorable game in Academy football were Richie Mayo and Bob Brickey. Four times Mayo was faced with 4th down and more than 6 yards to gain. To give up the ball was to admit defeat. Out came the words in the huddle, "Fish Hook Pass," and Brickey clutched the ball to his chest scant feet ahead of the down markers on four occasions. The game was won by a simple, well-timed pass pattern.

The routes of the two other receivers contribute much to the effectiveness of the primary receiver's course. The secondary routes in the pattern are run by the halfbacks and they tend to hold the short defender in the flat, which in turn permits the spread end to quickly reach an open spot.

Left Halfback

Set as the left wingback, the halfback starts in motion early and continues laterally into the opposite flat as the ball is snapped. He must make certain to get deep in the flat and remain on his side of the line of scrimmage until the pass is thrown. He should be about 6-8 yards deep in his own flat. This position will serve a dual purpose. The pattern will be well dispersed so that one defender cannot cover more than one receiver and the left halfback can act as a "safety valve" should the downfield men be covered.

Right Halfback

From his wingback position, the right halfback runs a "banana" route, so called because of its general appearance when drawn in a diagram. He forces downfield and slightly to the outside before rounding a course directly at the sideline at a depth of approximately 6 yards. This route tends also to hold a defender in the shallow flat and away from the spread end who is about to execute the fish hook route. The halfback's "out" route blends nicely with the curved "in" route of the spread end to make a fine 2-man pattern near the spot where the ball is to be thrown. It has the effect of a fast pace scissors upon a deep defender, freezing him long enough to assure the spread end of getting open for the short time necessary in a timing pass.

Variation

The fish hook principle can be applied to a drop-back pass as a weapon to hit a spot pass between linebackers in the short middle zone (7).

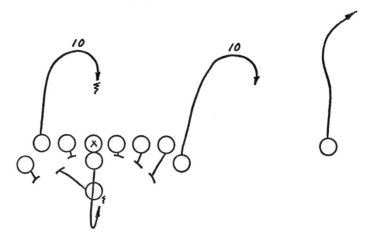

DIAGRAM 61.   Drop Back Fish Hook Pass.

The hooking left end runs a route behind the nearest linebacker and stops in the open zone between the two backers. The same pattern can be executed to the left for the wingback to become the primary target in the middle zone. The fish hook pattern can also be adapted to any defensive alignments including those with 3 and 4 linebackers stationed in the short zones.

Spread End Post

This fine 2-man pattern can be run equally as well from

drop-back style as from the quarterback roll-out fashion. The name *post* is given to the pattern although the spread end, who runs a route directly at the goal posts, is not the primary receiver. He clears out the area after forcing the defenders on his side into a man-for-man defense because of his extremely wide spacing. The right wingback is the number one target.

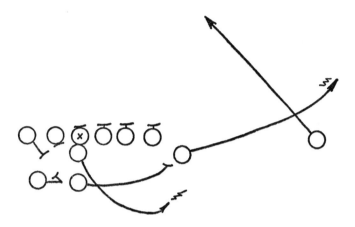

DIAGRAM 62.   End Post.

The spread end spaces to maximum distance laterally (18 yards) and runs a speed break straight at the goal posts. Between a depth of 8 and 12 yards, he looks in toward the quarterback, because if he's open at this time, the pass will come to him. He could break clear as the defense might attempt a delayed switch from their man-for-man coverage, and permit the spread end a step or two completely uncovered by a defender. The normal reaction is for the deep defender, who has covered off on the spread end, to start back and in with the end and then switch to covering the flaring wingback. At the moment of the switching coverage, one of the two receivers is open.

The right halfback, flaring out from his wingback, is the receiver who is usually open in the short zone (up to 12 yards) and he has caught many post patterns from the quarterback. Some have gone all the way for scores.

The wingback's course is virtually a great circle route aimed at a spot 3 yards in front of the spread end's starting point. He runs at full speed to outrun any short-defender who may have flat zone responsibility, and to break away from any man-for-man coverage in the deep secondary. After acquiring running room to the outside, the right halfback circles downfield looking over his inside (left) shoulder, for at this time the ball will be in the air. The ball is thrown when the wingback has only 5 yards of depth; but he is led downfield and the pass completion is usually made at 10 yards. Because of the speed of both receivers in the pattern, this play can break away for long gains although aimed to be a 10-yard pass.

Note: The same post route can be run from the short side with a wide flanker running the goal post route and the fullback running the flaring route of the primary receiver.

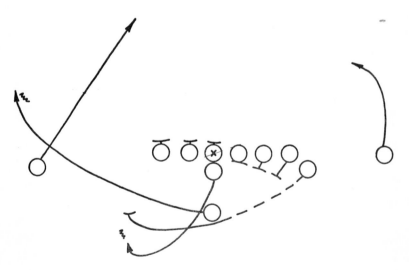

DIAGRAM 63.   Flanker Post.

Flood

The roll-out, or sprint-out, technique lends itself ideally to flooding a zone.

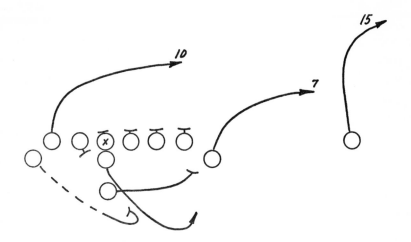

DIAGRAM 64. Flood Pattern (Strong Side).

There are three possible receivers, with the right halfback, from his wingback position, being the number one target as he runs a sideline break at an average depth of 6 yards. His is a timing route and he expects the ball within a step or two after veering toward the sideline. This timing and spot passing gives the defense very little time to adjust to directional flow or to distinguish between the threat of the quarterback's running pressure and a pass. The quarterback must be ready to throw the ball quickly after running away from center and gripping the ball for a pass.

The shortside end's pattern makes possible a throw-back receiver for the quarterback in the event the linebackers flow too swiftly toward the main body of the flood pattern. The angle may appear difficult but it is not, mostly because the distance is relatively short, and all the passer need remember is that he and the left end are on parallel courses at practically the same speed. The pass should be thrown directly at the receiver under these conditions with no lead distance figured. The quarterback's lateral motion will provide all the lead necessary for an accurate pass.

Note: The same flood pattern can be run to the short side with the right halfback, from his wingback position, flying back in motion and helping in the pass protection to the short side.

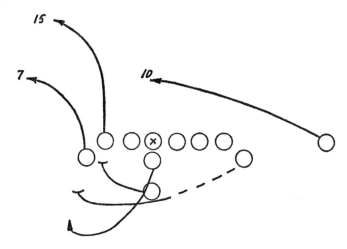

DIAGRAM 65.   Flood Pattern (Short Side).

The fish hook, post, and flood patterns are the fundamental patterns of the roll-out pass offense. The basic patterns of the drop-back cup style of passing follow. Since most roll-out patterns were detailed to the long side, the cup-style passes will be shown as flanker patterns, although they, too, can be directed at the unbalanced strong side of the line.

Cross

The cross pattern is a simple two-man pattern in which one

receiver dashes deep through a zone, clearing it for a partner who breaks sharply into the zone from the inside an instant after the spot has been swept clean.

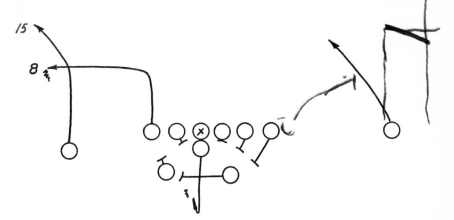

DIAGRAM 66.   Cross Pattern.

The flanking left halfback spaces at minimum or medium width in an effort to maintain a basic zone-type coverage among the opponents. (Very wide spacing invites a man-for-man coverage.) The desired zone coverage is more easily attacked with a medium depth (10 yards) pattern as the defenders tend to concentrate on the deep outside man and cover the medium depth receiver a bit more loosely.

The halfback sprints straight downfield to a depth of 12 yards, then breaks toward the sidelines at a 45 degree angle. This veer in direction will break him into the clear if the defense tries a switching coverage on the 2-man pattern. The flanker's job is to clear the zone for the left end's route; but should the switch be effected, the flanker would become the logical receiver. In a switch move, the man defending the flanker would back up with him until the end broke out beneath the flanker, then the defender would leave the flanker and pick up the end, leaving the flanker to his defending partner, the

safety man. The 45 degree sideline break will adequately take
the flanker away from the defensive safety man.

The shortside (left) end goes straight down the field for
8 yards, running under control. At this point he breaks at 90
degrees toward the sidelines and proceeds at full speed to take
a lead pass from the quarterback. The 6-count timing of a drop-
back pass will put the ball in the air so as to be caught by the
end 2 or 3 steps after making his break.

Criss-Cross

This play supplies to the total pass offense a pattern that is
sorely needed to prevent the defense from reacting only to
out-breaking and stop routes, which are the mainstays of the
possession pass attack. It involves two receivers, from opposite
flanks, running routes that cross somewhere near the center of
the secondary. The main target is still hit on spot timing at a
depth no greater than 12 yards.

The spread end runs a modified post route, not bending in
quite as much as he takes back the deep defender on his side.

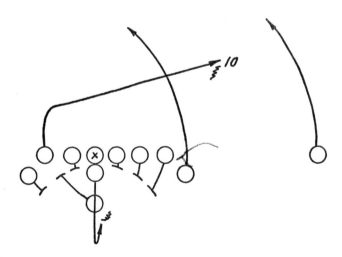

DIAGRAM 67. Criss-Cross.

The right halfback, from the wingback position, runs directly through centerfield as he clears out the deep middle zone defenders. He provides one part of the criss-cross pattern while the prime receiver, the left end, crosses paths with him. The shortside end is the more shallow of the two and has a clear zone into which to run. The left end's route takes him about 4-5 yards past the line of scrimmage, then he turns approximately 75 degrees to the right and sprints underneath the clearing right halfback to a spot 10-12 yards deep directly in front of the wingback's original position.

Rainbow

Having outlined one 2-man pattern and one 3-man pattern, it is appropriate to detail one 4-man pattern. Of course, the more receivers who are active in a pattern, the less protection that is afforded the passer. Any pattern that involves more than three receivers should not be undertaken unless the defense is rushing fewer than a usual number of men. The rainbow pattern involves both ends and both halfbacks with the left

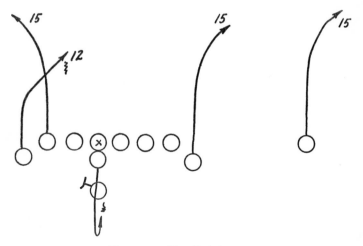

DIAGRAM 68. Rainbow.

halfback being the primary target of the passer. It is particularly effective against a 3-deep defense because it throws 4 receivers deep against the secondary.

The two ends run deep (15 yards) flag routes, taking the deep outside defenders with them. The right halfback runs a deep bending-out course which is a modified flag route. He normally will take the safety man with him. The left halfback runs straight down the field from his wingback spot trailing the shortside end by a stride until the end makes his break to the outside. At this point (12-15 yards) the left half bends in (like a rainbow) to the deep middle zone, which isn't easily attacked without a 4-man pattern. The ball is put into the air at his break to the inside. Only a double wing formation can pop 4 receivers deep quick enough to complete a timing pass.

Fullback Swing

The final pattern which rounds out the possession attack is a 5-man special to be used against a relatively slow-rushing defense employing 4 or less rushers. It can also be used as a naked screen pass to break the fullback loose behind a 2-man flood to either side.

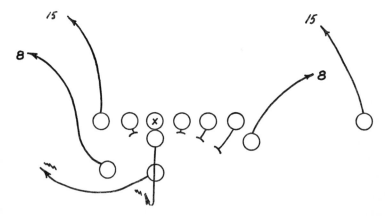

DIAGRAM 69.   Five   Man   Pattern.

Each side is a separate 2-man pattern involving an end and a halfback. The 5-man pattern is particularly effective when run to the short side where the halfback runs a flaring route from his normal halfback position. With one backfield man getting into the pattern from his regular position, it comes quite unexpectedly to the defense to have a second back appear to that side as a pass receiver. The fullback runs a quick swing route, bowing back to a depth of 7 yards before angling wide toward the line of scrimmage. His increased depth gives the quarterback a better passing angle as the fullback catches a soft pass over his inside (right) shoulder and turns the corner.

COUNTER-PLAYS FOR THE PASSING GAME

Whenever a team makes full use of a passing offense, whether the pass be integrated into the entire attack or not, the offense must include counter-weapons to be used when the defensive team is expecting a pass. This axiom is particularly valid when part of the pass offense is the drop-back, or pure passing game, which makes no effort to conceal the intent to pass. Having clearly shown that he wants to pass, the quarterback can make full use of plays that start out as passes and end up as runs. In the Flexible T offense, the counter-plays for the passing game are the screen pass and the draw play.

The screen pass technique was fully covered in Chapter 7, as a part of the quarterback's responsibilities and need not be detailed again. Suffice it to say that the screen is an excellent weapon both in gaining yardage and in providing an implement to keep the defense honest when a pass is actually being attempted. A defensive player who is wary of the screen pass will not be completely effective when a true forward pass is thrown. The Flexible T, because it attacks from many different formations, recommends tossing the screen pass to both halfbacks and the fullback and to either the left or right. It has been found to be most effective to the short side where the greatest amount of pass-rushing pressure is also located.

The offense offers a screen to the shortside end from all three types of passing. This can readily be accomplished because the end protects for the passer on drop-back, roll-out, and action passes. The roll-out and play-action screen plays to the end take the shape of throw-back passes behind the line and are useful when extreme pressure is exerted from the off-side defenders.

Two throw-back screen passes to the left end are shown below:

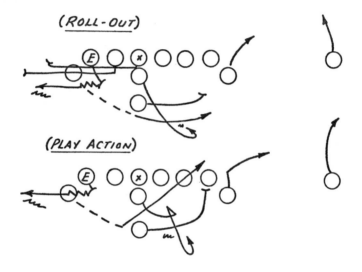

DIAGRAM 70.   Throw-Back Screens.

The other part of the counter-attack for the passing game, the draw play, has gained many valuable yards. These yards have not always been gained on a sure-passing down, either, but rather because the pass plays come at any time in the integrated attack. The draw play has been quite successful when used on the unusual passing situations. First-down draw plays have done extremely well.

The essence of the draw play is for the ball carrier to wait for the quarterback to bring the ball to him, then run to daylight. Since the backs are constantly drilled in the total offensive scheme to run to daylight, very little difficulty is encountered in teaching the daylight theory for the draw play. The coaching point to stress is waiting patiently for the quarterback to bring the ball to the carrier. Most ball carriers feel uncomfortable while standing still after the ball has been snapped. It *is* an unnatural reaction, but they must remain motionless until the ball is given to them. All the while, they should be watching the blocking pattern unfold in front of them so that a dash to daylight can be started immediately after the ball is tucked away.

The fullback draw play is executed from the drop-back style pass play and a definite blocking pattern is set up to increase the possibility of good daylight holes for the runner.

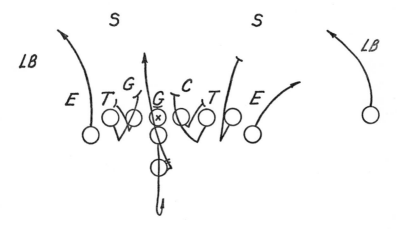

DIAGRAM 71. Fullback Draw.

The angle blocks of the guards help to clear the path effectively. The shortside end and inside tackle drop back the scissors to the inside to lead the interference. They help clean up on the center's man as required, or continue on for the linebackers. The fullback moves his left foot forward and to the right in a ¼ turn rotation, makes the ball pocket by raising his left elbow, and waits. With a good daylight runner, the fullback draw play may be expected to average close to 7 yards per try. It does for the Falcons.

The halfback draw play is executed from the roll-out style of pass play and the blocking assignments are set up to take advantage of the defense's tendency to react quickly with the directional flow of the roll-out action.

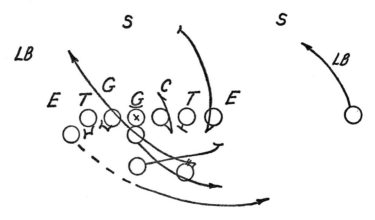

DIAGRAM 72.   Halfback Draw.

The center and tackles take their opponents in the direction of the roll-out, which is the direction they normally try to take anyway. The shortside guard turns out to seal off the pursuit and the right guard drops back one step then drives through on the nearest linebacker.

The fullback clears in front of the right halfback as he executes his normal roll-out type protection toward a point just outside of his strong tackle. This path helps to serve as a screen to hide the prospective ball carrier. The right halfback lines up ½ yard deeper than normal, permitting the fullback to pass easily in front of him and also giving himself a better view of the blocking pattern up ahead. He presents the ball pocket to the quarterback by lifting his left elbow and turning very slightly to the right, thus giving the quarterback a good target as he waits. Upon receiving the ball, the halfback runs to daylight in the general direction of the shortside guard. This course allows him to attack away from the flow of most of the defenders, against the grain, with an excellent opportunity to break away.

20

Reviewing the Flexible T

ONE APPROACH to offensive football has been set forth in this book. That approach has not assumed any superiority of manpower. As a matter of fact, the offense was designed with the specific object in mind of giving a team of below-average physical ability all of the weapons necessary to move the ball against a stronger opponent. A really concentrated effort was made to simplify the attack while retaining the inherent flexibility of the over-all system. Underlying the entire assortment of offensive weapons is the principle of maneuverability, which has been the smaller team's stock in trade since history began. An effort was made to give the attacking team the opportunity to call its own shots by flexing and deploying to control the defensive opponent.

The natural way of playing the game was endorsed to permit the players to be relieved of the additional strain of trying to execute a task to which they were unequal. Blockers were allowed, even directed, to block a defender in the direction of least resistance. No one was required to force a man aligned to his outside to move to his inside, especially if he did not want to go that way! Ball carriers were advised to run to daylight, or naturally, where there were the fewest number of enemy troops. Effort was put forth by the staff of coaches to evaluate the natural abilities of the players and then present to those players all of the weapons required to fully exploit their own skills before attempting to teach them any new, or unnatural, ones. Much time was spent in selecting the players for the team as it was accepted that the team would only be as good as were the players who comprised it. Know the players as people and then, and then *only,* will the staff be in a position to get the best out of them in the drive toward victory.

The specific approach recommended after being proved successful in advancing the ball was to establish the ground attack first. Then the passing game was developed, sold to the players as being effective and not dangerous, and then integrated with the running plays to form the balanced attack. The passing game was never to be considered as an emergency weapon.

Many weapons in the form of play series and specific pass patterns were developed. All plays could be run from various formations with the explanation that deploying with an unbalanced line, flankers, spread ends, wingbacks, line spacing and men-in-motion were all additional weapons to be used in controlling the defense. The plays plus the formations could be welded together to gain an advantage over an opponent, who, if not flexed, would prove utlimately superior because of greater strength and individual ability. Teamwork was stressed.

The play series were designed to complement each other and give to the entire system a balance of play types. The running series included the finesse, deception and option sweeps of the belly series as well as the generated power of the drive series with its massed attack and double team blocking assignments. Also included were the extremely quick-hitting plays of the trap series. Balance was also sought within each series as provision was made for counter-plays and action pass plays to augment the bread-and-butter mainstays. All basic styles and techniques of blocking at the point of attack were built into the system.

Just as the team required many weapons to conquer all sorts of resistance, the players performing at the attack point were given all the techniques necessary to handle any particular situation. They could handle an opponent in a man-for-man situation, acquire assistance in the form of a double team partner, set up their opponent for a lateral block from a trapping teammate, or execute a very special technique in the manner of the reverse-influence-and-switch block as used by the left end in 29 Reverse Belly.

The pass offense, which was to be an integral part of the system, was a spot type involving the short pass as a basic, but with provision being made for a really long scoring pass as dictated by the strategical situation. Individual routes were outlined in order to attack any specific zones with emphasis placed upon avoiding interception areas. A complete repertoire of more complete patterns involving from 2 to 5 potential receivers were provided for use under certain conditions.

The three main styles of pass protection were included: cup, roll-out and play-action as well as the techniques required of all of the protectors. Counter-plays for the passing game were presented in the shape of screen passes and draw plays. Coaching points to stress in each play series were underlined in an effort to avoid making mistakes when they really counted—in games.

Efficiency of the use of all of the weapons was emphasized with the purpose definitely *not* to use all of the weapons in any one game (unless absolutely necessary). The running plays which are not well-defensed should be used, and repeatedly so, until shut off by the opponent. When efficiency drops off, and only then, a new play or series should be employed. The same efficiency is desired in the use of the integrated pass plays. Nothing is proved when a team attacks directly at the strength of an opponent. The usual result is the relinquishing of the football. All defensive alignments have strengths and weaknesses built into them and a thorough understanding of this principle is a must for the attacking field general.

Much space in this book was devoted to the development of a quarterback and there can be no better way than that to insure an efficient use of the Flexible T offense. The quarterback must know his people, his weapons on offense, and have a real knowledge of defensive football if he is to attack an opponent intelligently, systematically and with efficiency. Not a single play should be wasted unless the odds favor taking the chance of a wasted down because of a special situation on the field which might result in a score and would not indicate giving up possession ahead of a normal schedule.

The attack can be varied by the quarterback by change of pace or the basic timing required for the ball to cross the line of scrimmage. This aspect is built into the offensive system in the various play series and the quarterback is advised to use the change of pace as a weapon as well as the other flexible items at his disposal: formations, backfield patterns, counters, styles of blocking at the point of contact, and the three types of pass patterns.

The Flexible T offense has the capability to move the ball, as has been evidenced by its performance during the first three years of use against major opponents across the nation. The system has averaged well over 300 yards gained from scrimmage in each game. Constant practice and rehearsal of the patterns and plays to perfect timing and unity, along with individual drills that simulate game conditions, will give any team the weapons needed to attack successfully.

Index